GETTIN
NAUTICAL IN
NEW ENGLAND

MAINE, NEW HAMPSHIRE, MASSACHUSETTS, RHODE ISLAND, CONNECTICUT

DANIEL SEDDIQUI

SCHIFFER
PUBLISHING

4880 Lower Valley Road • Atglen, PA 19310

Other Schiffer Books by the Author:
Jammin' through the South: Kentucky, Virginia, Tennessee, Mississippi, Louisiana, Texas, 978-0-7643-6748-9

Other Schiffer Books on Related Subjects:
New England Lighthouses: Famous Shipwrecks, Rescues, & Other Tales, Allan Wood, 978-0-7643-4078-9
In My Footsteps: A Cape Cod Traveler's Guide, Second Edition, Christopher Setterlund, 978-0-7643-6667-3
Sketchbook Traveler New England, James Lancel McElhinney, 978-0-7643-6616-1

Cover design by Molly Shields
Interior layout by Beth Oberholtzer
Photos courtesy of Liz Johnson, Maine Island Kayak Co., front cover (*top*), 142; Melanie White, front cover (*bottom left*); Lucky Catch, front cover (*bottom center*); Discover Newport, front cover (*bottom right*); Will Zimmerman, back cover, 34–35; Melissa Cox, 6; Visit Portland, 8–9; EasyBuy4u (iStock), 26–27; Mary Barker, 42–43; Pgiam (iStock), 52–53; sphraner (Bigstock), 58; sorsillo (Bigstock), 59; See Plymouth, 60-61; DenisTangneyJr (iStock), 68–69, 90–91; j76n (iStock), 78–79; halbergman (iStock), 96-97; Discover Newport, 104–5; Kent Fuller, 122–3; SBWorldphotography (iStock), 132–3

Type set in Brevia/Cambria

ISBN: 978-0-7643-6892-9
ePub: 978-1-5073-0549-2
Printed in China

Published by Schiffer Publishing, Ltd.
4880 Lower Valley Road, Atglen, PA 19310
Phone: (610) 593-1777; Fax: (610) 593-2002
Email: info@schifferbooks.com; Web: www.schifferbooks.com

For our complete selection of fine books on this and related subjects, please visit our website at www.schifferbooks.com. You may also write for a free catalog.

Schiffer Publishing's titles are available at special discounts for bulk purchases for sales promotions or premiums. Special editions, including personalized covers, corporate imprints, and excerpts, can be created in large quantities for special needs. For more information, contact the publisher.

THE IMMERSIVE TRAVEL GUIDE

Connect with local experts. Learn their artistry. Understand something meaningful to the region. Craft a piece of history.

This travel guide is something special. You're not just visiting a place—rather, you are *being in* a place. Take it from me, your guide, Daniel Seddiqui. I have been through the fifty states well over twenty times, and it never gets old. Engaging with new people, creating authentic experiences, and building newfound knowledge makes travel feel alive. From the start, I've envisioned a layout of the map (now Google Maps)—made of dots of cities and lines of highways—to become a reality, a life I call "Living the Map." My strategy of travel has always been to get to the heart of the people of a place and to learn how the natural environment inspires their innovation. I've spent decades identifying regional cultures to target for exclusive themes of experiences and developing a network to make opportunities available. From shooting archery with Cherokee Indians and building furniture with Amish craftsmen to cutting timber with Oregon lumberjacks, the memories I've made through experiential travel never fade and the relationships never dwindle, no matter how old I age.

To help bolster the meaning for travel, this book places a focus on Take It and Make It experiences. The Take It portion is about taking a lesson or joining in an activity, whether that is an instructed course or a leisurely pastime reflecting an area's local industry or culture. The Make It component is about handcrafting iconic symbols that the local artisans value, inspiring the traditional legacies and stories that we call America's craftsmanship. You'll learn new skills and have pieces of the region's pride to bring home with you.

—*Daniel Seddiqui*

MAINE

O Bangor

Augusta
★

Portland
O

Wells

VERMONT

NEW
HAMPSHIRE

Concord
★

Portsmouth

Gloucester

Boston
★

Provincetown

NEW

YORK

MASSACHUSETTS

Plymouth

Springfield O

Providence
★

Wareham

Hyannis

Nantucket

Newport

Hartford
★

CONNECTICUT

*Martha's
Vineyard*

RHODE
ISLAND

Mystic

Greenwich

NEW
JERSEY

CONTENTS

INTRODUCTION

Along Interstate 95, the waters of the Atlantic have drawn a rich culture for New England, where everyday life is steeped in tradition. Here, you'll find three centuries of the finest achievements in American architecture, decorative arts, and landscape design—spanning from the colonial era to the Gilded Age to modern day. The region is studded with high-caliber academia, including several Ivy League institutions, and it's a hub of storied American pastimes, such as baseball and basketball. This was the destined land for the colonists, where life on and around the waters was cherished, and—long after the American Revolution—New England's charms have inspired generation after generation to stay.

New England is tiny yet mighty, and exploring the region is like finding an unpacked treasure chest deep in the ocean, preserved and pristine. The old wooden dock pilings bracing a long pier are an invitation to explore the natural amenities of coastal New England. Lighthouses safely guide vessels into the harbors, lobstermen crank traps marked with buoys, synchronized rowers paddle through the coves, and sailors race the choppy bay waters. Wherever there's a dock, there's a boat eagerly waiting to be taken for an adventure, an escape, and life beyond the horizon. These wakes will drift you through Portland's fishing wharves, to the historic harbor of the Boston Tea Party, to America's first landing at Plymouth Rock and to the prominent islands of Martha's Vineyard and Nantucket. And, still, you're only halfway through! Maybe New England isn't so tiny after all. As you continue on, the yacht-filled harbors of Newport and the rowers at the Greenwich Water Club will introduce you to classic prestige and elitism.

To enrich your exploration of New England, learn how to make its iconic regional dishes, clam chowder and lobster rolls. Take a break from the water and take yourself out to the ballgame at the oldest baseball stadium in America, Fenway Park. Shop the antique trail in Maine's coastal town of Wells. Watch whales off the shores of New Hampshire and volunteer at a dolphin and whale conservation in Plymouth. Gamble at the largest casino in the country at Foxwoods Resort and try harvesting cranberries in Massachusetts and blueberries in Maine. And take home a custom-made paddle in New Haven. While there's plenty of resemblance to motherland England—such as the use of roundabouts and town names ending with the likes of -ham, -cester, and -ford—New England has taken on a character of its own. Get ready to soak it all in. The waters are calling for you to get nautical.

CHAPTER 1

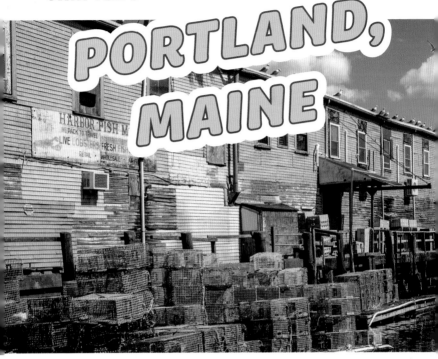

Finalizing a photo collage for a postcard of Portland would be difficult, because there are so many postcard-worthy scenes to consider. The many picturesque candidates include the rocky shores of crashing waves as a lighthouse peers down, the narrow brick alleys that navigate the old port, lengthy church spires, seagulls resting on retired rusty lobster traps, and the holiday wreaths that drape lampposts along the walkways. Portland, meaning land surrounding a harbor in Old English, is just that: a working port. The second-largest tonnage seaport in New England has turned

into one of America's finest romance cities. Enjoy window shopping along the brick-laid road on Exchange Street, hold hands on the docks of the marina, share a laugh ordering seafood on ice at a local restaurant, or venture to the shores for a sunset walk on the ocean sands.

Settled in 1632 and incorporated in 1786, Portland is a notable city, best known for its seafood restaurants, lighthouses, and nineteenth-century architecture. Nearby blueberry farms, moose sightings, and island hopping by ferry are also big draws.

Hang Out with the Locals

The accents of the locals are thick in Portland, and the dress code is modern-day Old England: suspenders, tight pants, and a fedora. Of course, that's for the local hipsters.

The lobstermen's attire is a tad different; you'll see them wearing orange waterproof overalls and thick nonslip boots. The accents are still there, and the toughness is authentic. For a genuine taste of Portland, catch your own lobster on a boat. Try anything not to get seasick, because the boat won't turn around.

TAKE IT

Catch your dinner with **Lucky Catch Cruises**— *170 Commercial Street*

Nearly every person worldwide associates lobster with the state of Maine. Lobster is not just a delicacy but a large part of the state's cultural and economic identity. Don't be surprised to see lobster themes throughout the region, and to truly comprehend its significance, it's a must to get out on a boat to appreciate and understand the hard work of those in the industry. Lucky Catch Cruises offers an open invitation to experience the daily life of a lobster fisherman. Enjoy getting out onto the waters of Casco Bay for an excursion of hauling up traps. The crew members allow you to have a hands-on experience and do as the professionals do. And, if you'd rather sit back and observe, soaking in the picturesque scenery of lighthouses, historic Civil War forts, and seal sightings, you don't have to feel like you're extra weight on the boat.

Each of the lobster tours lasts for eighty to ninety minutes, and passenger numbers are limited to ensure that everyone gets

an up-close and personal Maine lobstering experience. You'll see how these tasty treats get from the bottom of the ocean to your dinner plate, and learn about lobster habits, conservation efforts, and the differences among hard shells, shedders, shorts, culls, and keepers. Any lobsters you catch can be purchased after the cruise for wholesale "boat" price, and if you don't have a pot at home, you can take them across the pier to the Portland Lobster Company restaurant for the freshest lobster dinner anywhere.

A variety of marine life will enter a lobster trap, and some common visitors include rock crabs, snails, starfish, and hermit crabs. Lucky Catch Cruises has a see-through "live tank" that offers visitors a chance to watch these little creatures until the end of the day, when all are thrown back into the sea.

Lobster, fresh caught from the trap on the Atlantic. *Courtesy of Lucky Catch*

THE STORY OF *LUCKY CATCH'S* CAPTAIN

In 1984, Captain Tom's lobstering career began as a summer job for his neighbor Andy Strout. Off the beautiful rocky shores of Cape Elizabeth, they learned how to set lobster traps from a 23-foot boat, and when Tom reeled up his first "lucky catch," he was hooked.

"It was always a thrill to discover what was waiting inside the next trap," Tom recalls. "I guess that's the reason it's still enjoyable today."

The following summer, Tom began working for Andy's brother Frank on the 36-foot *Nancy J.*, which docked in Portland Harbor. Frank was a professional lobsterman, working full time year-round, and showed Tom the challenges and rewards of making a living on the sea. "Frank was the perfect role model," Tom explains. "He's a great fisherman, works hard, [and is] very knowledgeable, honest, and fair."

Tom had a vision to get his own 21-foot boat, if he wanted to be in control of his own destiny by putting in as many or as few hours as he decided. He started building his own traps, and the job requires many of them, since he was soon hauling up lobsters by hand.

A few years later he replaced the 21-foot boat with a 30-foot lobster boat named *Sue-Anna-Jean*. "Thankfully that boat had a hydraulic trap hauler," Tom mentions. In 1996, the 37-foot *Lucky Catch* was purchased to add size and stability but also to take on a new approach. During the summer months, Captain Tom began taking passengers out to tend his traps. On the one-and-a-half-hour excursions, guests experience the routines of a real Maine lobsterman. In December 2007, the new 40-foot *Lucky Catch* was launched in Northeast Harbor, Maine. It carries passengers in the summer but lobsters commercially the remainder of the year.

Demonstrating how to handle a live lobter is lobsterman Brian Vibes.
Courtesy of Lucky Catch

TIPS ON HOW TO AVOID SEASICKNESS

For some it's inevitable, for others it's a fleeting moment, but most everyone agrees that getting seasick is one of the worst feelings of helplessness. The rolling waves, whether subtle or ripping, make your head spin and your stomach turn. There are approaches to avoiding this feeling, but sometimes just not going out on the water is the best option.

Get Fresh Air

Sometimes, just the smell alone can make you queasy, whether it's the fuel exhaust or the fishy atmosphere. Try to catch some of the breeze, and inhale the freshness of the air when you can. Exhaust from the engine is almost unavoidable, so stay as far away as possible from that side of the boat. Experts also say that any strong smells such as perfume can cause nausea. It's best to stay away from enclosed spaces, because they capture that nasty stale air you want to avoid.

Try to Relax

Keep yourself occupied by staying busy with an activity, such as cranking up traps or hoisting sails. Anxiety is a huge contributor to seasickness, so try listening to music. Last, board with confidence, rather than expecting to feel sick. Try to enjoy the natural elements and breathe deep to relax your negative thoughts.

Keep the Horizon in Sight

They say that seasickness can be triggered in and around fog. Getting lost in a daze can really mess up your internal compass. So, if you can't see out into the horizon, keep your eyes closed. This will reduce the conflicting signals between your eyes and inner ear. Your body needs to adjust to the boat's motion, so finding stable points of reference helps reduce dizziness. Don't use binoculars or cameras or read for an extensive length of time, and avoid staring at close objects that your brain would usually consider stable; this will only make your symptoms worse.

Manage Your Diet

Keeping your stomach empty does not help avoid vomiting. You know your body better than anyone, so understand the foods that typically agree with you. Make sure you're eating foods that are easy on the stomach, so avoid things that are spicy, acidic, and fatty. Definitely do not overeat, and make sure you're hydrating before and during the excursion. Experts say that peppermint and ginger are natural remedies to seasickness and can be added to your meals throughout the day. Experts also suggest not consuming too much alcohol before boarding.

Stay Out of Direct Sun

Even when you're on land, direct sun for too long can cause headaches and fatigue. You want to keep your body from overheating, so take shelter under shade often.

Bring Medicine and Other Helpful Products

Talk to your doctor before you go out on the water and come prepared with medicine they recommend to help manage seasickness. Popular over-the-counter recommendations are Dramamine and Bonine. It's suggested that you take the medicine twenty-four hours before boarding so it's more effective in your bloodstream.

Many avid boaters, paddlers, and sailors recommend that those who are prone to seasickness or who feel anxious about seasickness try Psi bands, which are adjustable wristbands that apply acupressure. Designed to relieve nausea and vomiting, these bands can be found at the pharmacy and are worth a try. Unfortunately, they do not always work for everyone.

Transderm Scop motion sickness patches help prevent nausea and vomiting from motion sickness with minimal side effects but do need a prescription. You simply apply the patch behind your ear, and it will last for up to three days. As with any medication, talk to your doctor first before using.

Portland Regency Hotel & Spa—
20 Milk Street

Rich with local history, Portland Regency Hotel & Spa is located in a nineteenth-century, neoclassical armory building—a historic landmark in Portland's Old Port District, just two blocks from the waterfront. The porte cochere, known as the drop-off zone, is worth noting because of its historical design, using cobblestones circling a rotary or roundabout. The "State of Maine Armory," as it was called, was built for Maine's National Guard in 1895 at a cost of $20,000. At the time, it was considered one of the finest and best-equipped armories in New England. In 1941, the armory became vacant when the federal government took control of Maine's National Guard troops. City officials ultimately decided to open the armory to house soldiers, sailors, and marines who were temporarily stranded in Portland. During one two-month period, over four thousand men took advantage of the facility for overnight stays.

In 1942, the United States Navy took control of the armory and used it as a recreation center for the duration of World War II. At the close of the war, the building once again

served multiple purposes: as a home to the National Guard's citizen soldiers, as a civic auditorium, and as the city's public bathhouse. In 1962, the armory was taken over by the City of Portland for conversion into a waterfront parking lot. That would've been a huge mistake, but before this transformation could happen, the armory was sold to State Paper Company for use as a warehouse.

Stepping into this luxury hotel now, you couldn't imagine that all

of this took place in the building's history. Currently, it's one of the area's most elegant properties; as they say, "Portland Regency welcomes you with both traditional grandeur and a very contemporary sense of convenience and style. You'll feel at ease the moment you step across the cobblestones and into our open lobby, with its elegant staircase and timeless grace."

During your stay, be sure to try the hotel's phenomenal restaurant and bar called the Armory Lounge. This quintessential New England underground ambience can't be mistaken for any other place. It's cozy and has a studious feel—like you're at study tables in a library. The food is local and so are many of the drinks.

Inside the Portland Regency is the underground lounge, called the Armory. *Courtesy of Visit Portland*

A Regional Staple: Lighthouses

The coast of Maine is decorated with lighthouses, from every tip of land and edge of the islands. They're a symbol of the state, but what are they used for? The National Ocean Service explains:

> Lighthouses are towers with bright lights and fog horns located at important or dangerous locations. They can be found on rocky cliffs or sandy shoals on land, on wave-swept reefs in the sea, and at entrances to harbors and bays. They serve to warn mariners of dangerous shallows and perilous rocky coasts, and they help guide vessels safely into and out of harbors. The messages of these long-trusted aids to navigation are simple: either **STAY AWAY, DANGER, BEWARE!** or **COME THIS WAY!**

The Spring Point Ledge Lighthouse, 2 Fort Road, South Portland, is accessible, giving visitors the rare opportunity to navigate the inside of an operating lighthouse. It's the only caisson-style light station in the United States that visitors can walk to. Located on the breakwater at Southern Maine Community College in South Portland, the lighthouse has been an integral part of the history of Portland Harbor and Casco Bay since 1897. The large boulders serving as a pier to the station create a beautiful setting, which fits the backdrop of Maine's rocky shores and tiny nearby islands.

If you're seeking to explore a more towering lighthouse that is postcard perfect, visit **Portland Head Light** at Cape Elizabeth, which is just 10 miles from the city center. Even the drive alone to get there is worth it, navigating windy quintessential New England neighborhoods and rolling grass hills like the countryside of Europe.

Walkway to the Spring Point Ledge Lighthouse. *Courtesy of Visit Portland*

The rocky shores with Portland Head Light
peering down. *Photo by Daniel Seddiqui*

MAKE IT

Learn to prepare lobsters like a local at **Luke's Lobster**—
60 Portland Pier

Ever wonder how a local prepares their lobster? Do they broil or boil? Do they drown it in butter? There are so many questions on what's the best way to get that delicious flavor and texture. Learn from the locals at **Luke's Lobster** at 60 Portland Pier. You've heard of farm-to-table food—how about boat-to-table? This establishment on the pier has contracted lobstermen to pull up at the docks and unload dozens of traps, filled with live lobsters. Luke's Lobster has a freshwater holding station, where the lobsters crawl and swim until a customer orders one.

 PREPARE LOBSTER LIKE THE LOCALS

This is how people from Maine commonly prepare lobster, whether at home or at a restaurant:

1. Do not just boil your lobsters in a big tub of water. True Mainers recommend steaming lobsters with 2 to 3 inches of water in the bottom of the lobster pot, preferably with a rack in the base.

2. Bring water to a rolling boil. Then drop live lobsters in head first (which is slightly more humane). Cover tightly with a lid. Watch for the water to return to a rolling boil—leave lobsters in for ten to fifteen minutes after water has come back to boiling. Remember, "Red is dead and done."

3. Drain the lobster and enjoy. Be sure to have melted butter, your bib, and a bucket for shells ready to go.

You should eat lobster on the same day as arrival, storing them in a cool place. They say don't cook a dead lobster, only live fresh ones. However, some lobster shippers say it is safe to cook and eat a lobster that passed in transit, recommending that you cook that lobster separately.

💡 HOW TO EAT LOBSTER

1. Order a fresh live Maine lobster.

2. Wear appropriate clothing, because things can get messy. Even consider wearing a bib!

3. Twist off the eight small legs with your hands, but be careful of the prickles that feel like a rose thorn. Suck out the meat and juices. Crunching down on the legs helps.

4. Twist off the claws. Crack the claws with a hinged nutcracker or a mallet, then take out the meat. Don't miss the slivers of meat in the claw's knuckles and "thumbs."

5. Gently twist off the tail from the body. Break off the flippers and treat them in the same manner as the small legs—there's tender meat there too. Now you can get the tail meat out. Place your thumb on the back of the tail where the flippers were and push hard. The tail meat will slide out the top. There's truly more meat than people might think!

6. Separate the back of the body and eat the green tomalley (optional). Crack the body open sideways and remove the last bits of meat. Congratulations! You now eat lobstah like a native Mainah!

TAKE IT

Become one with the waters with **Maine Island Kayak Co.**—
Kayak Beach, Peaks Island

If you've survived a lobster boat ride without getting sick, it's time for
more adventures on the water. Kayaking in Maine is a treat, but just
getting to your kayaking spot can be an adventure too. Taking a ferry
ride on the Casco Bay to one of the many islands is a must. Just a
seventeen-minute ride from downtown Portland, the Casco Bay Lines
at 56 Commercial Street will take you on a scenic ride to Peaks Island,
the special destination where you'll meet your kayak instructors.

⊙ WHILE YOU'RE HERE

Just a short twenty-minute drive from Portland through the rolling grass countryside, blueberry farms are scattered throughout the region. Maine's blueberries are the most iconic in the nation because the state produces 99 percent of all the blueberries in the country. Blueberries in Maine are "low bush," also known as wild blueberries, and **Dragonfly Meadow Blueberry Farm** at 1 West Lane in Arundel allows you to pick your own during the summer months. Bring a bucket, take pictures, and enjoy another one of Maine's signature treats. They can be used to make beverages and pies or even for a facial.

Treading waves on kayaks.
Courtesy of Liz Johnson,
Maine Island Kayak Co.

Paddle out to sea and become one with the waters. These are protected waterways with short but lively crossings, and there's the challenge of rock and surf. The kayak sits low, so you'll feel like you're treading through the waves. This is a one-of-a-kind experience, paddling the open ocean, near rocky cliffs and the lighthouses. You can't find views of islands like this in many other places in the US. Kayaks can be booked for a half day (three hours), a full day (five to seven hours), or a sunset ride (two hours). For details, visit www.maineislandkayak.com.

CHAPTER 2

WELLS, MAINE

It's not hard to see why Wells is a big draw for those who appreciate the art of antiquing, whether they're interested in nautical-themed pieces or other treasures. Just an hour south of Portland, there are well over twenty-five antique shops directly on Route 1, known as the Antique Trail. If you're searching for local vintage finds, including everything from jewelry, artwork, and furniture to sculptures, rare books, and much more, this region notably

has some of the nation's oldest pieces. Spend an hour or several exploring antique shops and meeting many of the local owners. As the state's third-oldest city, founded in 1643, Wells has turned into a popular summer destination because of its access to the beaches and resort-style accommodations and proves itself worthy of the title "the Friendliest Town in Maine."

Best Antique Shops on Route 1

People often judge the quality of a restaurant by how many cars are in the parking lot—and that same principle applies when assessing the antique shops in Wells. As you work your way along Route 1, be prepared to know which stores are worth exploring; otherwise, you could spend all day jumping in and out of the car. Here are a few suggested dealers, but keep in mind that many of the shops are close, so if you have that fear of missing out, you can still visit many others in a short period of time too.

Arundel Antique Village—*1713 Portland Road, Arundel*
This two-hundred-dealer antiques center offers a wide range of period antiques consisting of over 250 unique displays. It is considered Maine's busiest antiques mall. For information, call 207-985-7965.

One of many antique shops to browse, as you search for local gems

Wells Union Antiques—*Route 1, Wells*
Nine individually owned shops with fifteen dealers carry a wide range of country, formal, American, English, and Continental furniture, as well as paintings, and accessories. Also available are garden and architectural pieces, as well as glass, china, jewelry, and collectibles. The store is open seven days a week. Call 207-646-4551.

R. Jorgensen Antiques—*502 Post Road, Wells*
Eleven extensive showrooms feature fine period antiques; formal and country pieces; American, British Isles, French, and Scandinavian items; and furniture and accessories—all displayed in lovely room settings. Call 207-646-9444.

Bo-Mar Hall Antiques & Collectibles—*1622 Post Road, Wells*
One of the highest rated stores in Wells, where even locals frequently visit, this spot offers a vast array of antiques and collectables from over one hundred vendors all under one roof. They have flea markets on the weekends, depending on the weather. This location is one of the largest in the region, and some guests make a game of visiting the store with a scavenger hunt. Call 207-360-0943.

Wells General Store Antique Gifts—*2023 Post Road, Wells*
It's not always about the size of the store; it's about the quality. Reached via what seems like a private residential driveway, this site used to be home to a general store in 1842. They have large vintage road and commercial signs advertising gas and the general store. There is a Coca-Cola section, where it looks like you're stepping back into a 1950s diner. They are only open on weekends. Call 207-646-5553.

INTERVIEW WITH ANTIQUE DEALER TOM PRIOR OF ANYTIME ANTIQUES IN WELLS

What makes a great antique shop?

Cleanliness. We have four hundred to five hundred customers per day, touching items and moving them to different spots. We make sure to clean our products and every surface throughout the day.

What sets antique shops apart from one another? Is it inventory?

Customer service, actually. We care about our business and make sure we stay organized through the clutter. We always greet customers and teach them about the story behind how we obtain unique items. Our shop rents out space to vendors, and they are very knowledgeable about what they're selling.

What do people enjoy about antiquing?

The hunt. Whether you're a tourist or local, people are looking for a particular item more so than browsing. If you're a collector, you're trying to find that missing piece of a set. Our most popular sold item is furniture.

How did you get started in the business?

My dad was an auctioneer, so I saw the value of various items. I would skip school on Fridays and go antiquing with my dad. We always enjoyed the hunt and repurposing many items. I have run this place for twenty years, and I'm only thirty-seven years old.

TIPS ON BEING A SAVVY ANTIQUES SHOPPER

- **Know your terminology.** Experts say that an item should be at least one hundred years old and in original condition to be classified as "antique." (Motor vehicles are an exception to this rule, with some definitions requiring an automobile to be as little as twenty-five years old to qualify as "antique.") The majority of experts have agreed that items over fifty years old but less than one hundred years old can be called "vintage" or "collectible" but not "antique."

- **Negotiate the price.** Some dealers are firm, but antique shops are not like commercial retail chains. This is a perfect opportunity to practice your negotiating skills.

- **Check if the item is authentic.** You can always ask if there's a certificate of authenticity.

- **Ask questions about the item.** It's always good to know the story of the item's journey, because every item has a unique story. It's good to know where it came from, find out how it was made, and learn about its value.

- **Remember that antiques are not always functional.** Antiques can be used for decoration, as a keepsake, or for resale, so don't worry if it's not a functional household item.

- **Consider resale value.** Many people shop for antiques only to refurbish/refinish the item, so they can enjoy the process of increasing the value and reselling it.

TAKE IT

Discover the critters in a tide pool with **Coast Encounters**

A string of beaches runs through Wells from Drake's Island to Moody Beach. The strands of sand are lined with beachfront properties and rocky piers. If you just want to enjoy a little serenity on the Atlantic, with far fewer people than in Florida, pull up a lawn chair or put down a towel and soak up the sun. The beaches are popular during the summer months. You'll find people camping in tents, fishing from the beach, and tide-pooling. A local company, Coast Encounters offers excursions in tide pools.

People enjoy exploring the many tide pools of Maine, but do you actually know about the amazing critters that live between the tides? Coast Encounters will take you on a true, hands-on Maine adventure where you will roll up your sleeves and romp in the tide pools. Tide-pooling excursions are run daily (weather permitting) May through October in Kennebunk, Wells, or Ogunquit.

"If sitting on a boat for hours squinting to catch a glimpse of marine life doesn't appeal to you, you've come to the right place," explains Carol Steingart, otherwise known as "Coastal Carol." "You'll peek under rocks and seaweed, learn how to identify over thirty intertidal plants and animals, and use all five of your senses. And you'll learn how to explore the ecosystem in a way that is both safe and respectful to the wildlife living there. Plus, our excursions won't make you seasick!" You can learn more and reach Coastal Carol by visiting www.coastencounters.com.

Tide-pooling with Coastal Carol.
Courtesy of Carol Steingart

CHAPTER 3

PORTSMOUTH, NEW HAMPSHIRE

Settled in the early 1600s, the walkable seaport of Portsmouth shows the possibilities of what a prosperous city by the water looks like. Once one of the nation's busiest ports and shipbuilding cities, Portsmouth has one of the oldest working ports in the United States. The city planners realized that an active port, with tugboats escorting vessels, can be a huge draw for tourism. Now, Portsmouth's seaport is vibrant with visitors relishing the sights and sounds of

international trade while savoring a bite to eat or playing games near the waterfront at Prescott Park. The city prides itself on presentation, which is apparent in the well-maintained streets, and the buildings are lavish red brick, creating a modern facade. Portsmouth is at the center of the Seacoast Region, surrounded by tiny islands, naturally decorated with dense forest and rocky terrain, and easily accessible by car or boat, where over 20,000 residents call home.

TAKE IT

View the sea's majestic mammals with **Granite State Whale Watch**—*1870 Ocean Boulevard, Rye*

Since all whale watchers are "guests" visiting the natural environment of these animals, Granite State guides consider every whale watch tour a true expedition rather than a sightseeing excursion. Thus, your whale watch boarding pass is not an admission to a show but rather an opportunity to observe wild animals, which, on a worldwide basis, are quite rare. Whether you sight these marvelous creatures is entirely up to the whales, but the probability

is excellent—the tours have a 99 percent sighting record. On the rare occasion that they do not sight any whales or dolphins, a free pass good for one year will be issued.

Granite State Whale Watch is very fortunate to be located centrally to Jeffreys Ledge, where cold, nutrient-rich waters support a large variety of sea life, including zooplankton, krill, sand lance, herring, and mackerel—all of which are favorite foods for the whales. All of the company's whale watches travel to Jeffreys Ledge or the northern section of the Stellwagen Bank National Marine Sanctuary. During the past several years, Jeffreys Ledge has hosted the largest population of whales on the New England coast, and it attracts a large variety of marine mammals. On Granite State Whale Watch's expeditions, you have a chance of encountering 40-ton humpback whales, 70-foot finback whales, minke whales, and highly endangered right whales. Other species sighted include Atlantic white-sided dolphins, harbor porpoises, pilot whales, harbor seals, sharks, tuna, and ocean sunfish.

The company's whale watches are led by experienced and qualified naturalists who enjoy sharing their love of the marine environment with the passengers. On board are educational materials, kids' books, and posters, and the staff is always available for questions! To book your reservation, visit www.granitestatewhalewatch.com.

Visitors have the chance to see some of the Atlantic's majestic animal life on a whale watch. *Courtesy of Melanie White*

Portsmouth's walkable streets and lively restaurants along the active port serve up plenty of views of the water. *Courtesy of Will Zimmerman*

Exploring the Area

The Seacoast's Portsmouth has always been a fine destination for locals as a romantic getaway where peace and serenity are found. There are many cute, walkable streets and alleyways filled with gift shops and restaurants, with easy access to views of the water. The city offers an up-close experience with the region's history through maritime activities. This area is designed for breathtaking water views, whether cruising over bridges to island-hop or hopping on a cruise to experience sunrises or sunsets. Take a drive to New Castle Island on 1B Highway, which circles multiple islands, offering an opportunity to drive across multiple bridges, where you can explore the narrow residential neighborhoods and see the Portsmouth Naval Shipyard, the US Coast Guard, recreational boaters, and plenty of fishermen.

Back at Portsmouth Harbor, it's hard to miss those iconic Moran tugboats moored at Ceres Street. It is fascinating to watch as they escort a tanker up the Piscataqua River through one of the fastest currents in North America. Abundantly offered on the Seacoast are, once again, lighthouses, which tell a story, as do Great Bay, Little Bay, and the nine islands in the Isles of Shoals, just 6 miles off the coast of Portsmouth. If you make a quick trip to see the **USS *Albacore*** museum, you'll get an intimate experience learning about the research submarine that revolutionized the American version of the teardrop hull form of modern submarines. This can be found at 569 Submarine Way.

TAKE IT

Get in the water with **Portsmouth Scuba**—
915 Sagamore Avenue

You've gazed at the water and been on the water—but don't leave out being *in* the water. Portsmouth Scuba offers guided shore dives, an activity recommended for certified divers only—or those who are willing to invest in multiple days of training. Initiated on a teen's passion of finding "things," founder Jay wanted to turn a houseboat into a one-bedroom apartment. Due to zoning restrictions, the boat instead transformed into a dive shop and has been operating for over thirty-five years. When lifelong dedication and passion are proven, there's no better business to trust. All the equipment is provided to take a deep dive to look for sea life, including crabs, torpedo rays, squid, and bass. The business's mission manifests into a four-pillar dive program consisting of recreational dive training, local diving awareness, organized dive trips, and dive gear purchases and maintenance.

CHAPTER 4

GLOUCESTER, MASSACHUSETTS

Located on Cape Ann and home to the oldest seaport in the country, this city—pronounced "glawster"—is a waterfront haven tucked into Gloucester Harbor. With beaches, parks, restaurants, and a host of water activities and maritime museums, you can't ask for a better place

to enjoy not only historic landmarks but also "watermarks." Take in the ever-changing scenes, as the schooners drift the currents and the bells of the cathedrals ring. Gloucester commemorates its long history of fishermen, putting these rocky shores on the map.

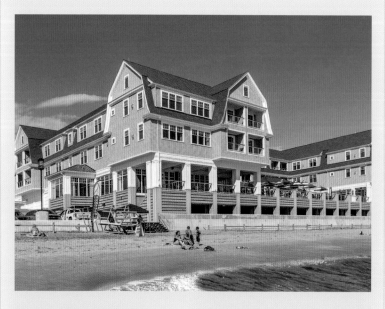

Beauport Hotel Gloucester—
55 Commercial Street
With a picturesque oceanfront location, upscale amenities, and unforgettable hospitality, the ninety-four-room Beauport Hotel Gloucester is the perfect getaway. Sitting on the oldest fishing port in America, Beauport Hotel Gloucester offers the peak Cape Ann experience. Enjoy its rooftop pool surrounded by harbor views, or take out a bicycle and pedal the waterfront parks or the narrow downtown streets.

Beachfront property. *Courtesy of Beauport Hotel*

Gloucester boasts a long history with the water. *Courtesy of Melissa Cox*

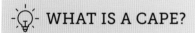 WHAT IS A CAPE?

Capes such as Cape Ann are commonly found in New England. Per *World Atlas*, there are two main features of a cape: there is a large portion of land that extends into a large water body such as an ocean, and there is a change both in the shape and the direction taken from the rest of the coastline. Capes are usually formed through volcanic activities, wave action, glaciers, and changes in the sea level. In any of these methods, erosion plays a significant role. A cape is not the same thing as a peninsula, which is a term that refers to a piece of land that is connected to the mainland, with water surrounding most of its border. However, a cape can be found at the end of a peninsula. Geologically, capes have short life spans because of the frequent erosion they undergo thanks to their proximity to any natural cause of erosion, especially tides.

MAKE IT

Learn how to repair ships at **Maritime Gloucester**—
23 Harbor Loop

Maritime Gloucester's campus has two distinct areas for visitors to enjoy. The pier is free and open to the public. On it, you will find America's oldest continuously operating marine railway, several historic wooden boats, the dory shop, and, in the summer, an oyster upweller operated by the Mass Oyster Project. There is an admission fee for the gallery and aquarium spaces. In this space, you will find an exhibit focused on the Stellwagen Bank National Marine Sanctuary, the Gorton's Maritime Gallery, the outdoor Sea-Pocket Aquarium, and the new Maritime Science Education Center. They also have a museum store, curated with a unique selection of gifts, books, toys, and clothing for kids and adults.

During your visit, you can learn about twisting twine to make a rope, and you can crank a foghorn and take in a demonstration of vessel maintenance. Maritime Gloucester offers apprenticeships in shipbuilding and repairs at its dory shop, but since you're just passing through, you can enjoy quick demonstrations on various topics ranging from traditional seamanship to diesel mechanics.

Just outside the dory shop sits a vessel.
Courtesy of Maritime Gloucester

Historic schooners out on tour.
Courtesy of Mary Barker

TAKE IT

Step back in time at **Gloucester Marine Railways**—
81 Rocky Neck Avenue

If you're seeking an observational experience in a working shipyard, Gloucester Marine Railways offers a firsthand look at hauling out vessels like it was done in the 1800s. The Gloucester Harbor had a booming fishing industry, but there were not many places that repaired and restored working ships. Since 1859, the Rocky Neck Marine Railways, now known as the Gloucester Marine Railways Corp., has maintained and repaired thousands of fishing, commercial, and pleasure boats, from the wooden schooners of the last century to the present-day steel and fiberglass vessels. Watch how the boats are cranked up on a cradle and lifted onto railroad tracks, where the ships can be repaired. Book a tour with general manager Donald King by calling 978-317-1622 or emailing office@gmrailways.com.

 WHILE YOU'RE HERE

As you drive out of Gloucester and head toward Boston, you'll pass through Salem, Massachusetts, after just 17 miles along the route. This city was the site of the infamous Salem Witch Trials. In 1692 to about midway through 1693 in colonial Massachusetts, more than two hundred people were accused of practicing witchcraft. As detailed by literature presented by Salem Witch Museum,

> In January of 1692, nine-year-old Betty Parris and eleven-year-old Abigail Williams, the daughter and niece of Salem Village minister Reverend Samuel Parris, suddenly feel ill. Making strange, foreign sounds, huddling under furniture, and clutching their heads, the girls' symptoms were

alarming and astounding to their parents and neighbors. When neither prayer nor medicine succeeded in alleviating the girls' agony, the worried parents turned to the only other explanation[:] the children were suffering from the effects of witchcraft. As word of the illness spread, others began to fall ill with the same alarming symptoms. The afflicted complained disembodied spirits were stabbing them, choking them, and jabbing them with pins. Soon names were cried out as the afflicted began to identify these specters. Neighbors, acquaintances, and total strangers were named in the statements and examinations that followed.

These events resulted in the largest series of witchcraft trials to ever take place in North America, and they marked the last large-scale witch panic to take place in the English colonies. All told, between 150 and 200 people were jailed for witchcraft, and fourteen women and five men were hanged, while one man was tortured to death and at least five people died in prison. To learn more about these events, visit the **Salem Witch Museum** at 19½ Washington Square North, Salem.

Salem Witch Museum. *Courtesy of Mary Barker*

CHAPTER 5

BOSTON, MASSACHUSETTS

There's no escaping the ever-aging history in New England, and while the world-class city of Boston keeps pace with the modernizing world, the city respects its past by preserving buildings and parks, traditions, and industries. Boston is the living encyclopedia of America—an education hub exploring subjects of science, history, sports, politics, fine arts, and medicine. It's no wonder that dozens of colleges and universities have made

Boston their home. Not many cities in America have as many recognizable sites as Boston, including Faneuil Hall, Boston Commons, Quincy Market, Copley Square, Commonwealth Avenue, Bunker Hill, Fenway Park, Newbury and Boylston Streets, and Boston Harbor. With its storied past and modern present, Boston can confidently claim legend status.

TAKE IT

Reenact history at **Boston Tea Party Ships & Museum**—
306 Congress Street

One of the nation's most pivotal moments in history was the Boston Tea Party, when colonists displayed their opposition of the taxation without representation on goods from Britain. On the night of Thursday, December 16, 1773, the "tea crisis" in Boston came to a head. Members of the Sons of Liberty disguised themselves as Mohawk Indians and were armed with an assortment of axes. They quietly boarded three ships, which were moored at Griffin's Wharf and carrying cargoes of British East India Company tea. In a span of three hours, 340 chests of British East India Company tea were smashed and dumped into Boston

Visitors to Boston Tea Party Ships &
Museum can reenact throwing tea
crates into Boston Harbor. *Courtesy
of Michael Blanchard Photography /
Boston Tea Party Ships & Museum*

Harbor. Over 92,000 pounds of tea was destroyed and thrown
into the harbor. The implications and impact of the Boston Tea
Party were enormous; the event directly led to the sparking of
the American Revolution on April 9, 1775.

This historic site on Boston Harbor allows guests to step
onto replica ships, reenact throwing tea overboard, and enjoy
the tea-tasting room. The original teas include Colonial Bohea,
Congou Tea, Young Hyson Tea, Lapsang Souchong Tea, and Singlo
Tea. Take a seat with a costumed interpreter of a colonist and
enjoy the tastes of the eighteenth century.

Take a tour of the museum and see the many artifacts from
the Boston Tea Party, which even include an original tea chest
found at the bottom of the harbor.

 WHILE YOU'RE HERE

Boston is saturated with historical buildings, statues, and roadways. If
you want to continue discovering historic events and sites that include
reenactments, **the Freedom Trail** maps a route to seventeen locations
over 2.5 miles that have changed the course of American history. Visit
www.thefreedomtrail.org for more information on doing a scheduled or
self-guided tour.

🏨 CHECKING IN

Boston Harbor Hotel—
70 Rowes Wharf
Every step inside the Boston Harbor Hotel is set to impress. After walking inside, you'll find a grand, elegant entrance with gracious staff ready to serve. There are several restaurants that will take your breath away, all capturing the stunning views of Boston Harbor. You can't miss teatime, a signature feature keeping history and traditions alive from the days of the colonists. And, of course, the rooms are clean, modern, and inviting. You won't want to leave your room; the views of Boston Harbor from your bedside are the idyllic urban experience, allowing you to watch yachts going in and out and planes flying gradually into the airport.

Viewed from Boston Harbor, the Boston Harbor Hotel is a modern addition to the city's skyline.
Courtesy of Boston Harbor Hotel

⊙ WHILE YOU'RE HERE

Experience the epicenter of academia during your stay in Boston. There are many universities and colleges based in Boston—forty-four to be exact. Plus, there are dozens more in the metro area. Many institutions welcome visitors for tours of their campuses, including lecture halls, performing arts venues, and athletic fields, stadiums, and arenas. The best known are Massachusetts Institution of Technology (MIT), Harvard University, Tufts University, Boston College, Boston University, Northeastern University, and Suffolk University. It is said that Boston is the smartest city in the country, and these tours offer perspectives of student life, refer to historical events on campus, highlight great discoveries made by students and professors, and discuss newer developments and visions.

While college campus tours are usually the domain of prospective students and accompanying family members, some institutions are worth exploring by anyone who appreciates tradition, architecture, and achievement. Head to **Harvard University**

(1350 Massachusetts Avenue, Cambridge) to experience the ideas, artifacts, people, and places that have shaped the storied university's history for nearly four hundred years. Harvard is the most prestigious university in America, and it is regarded as the pinnacle of educational influence. The campus offers history tours by current Harvard students, which last between forty-five and sixty minutes. If you've always been curious about how Harvard became world class and continues to pave the way of the future, questions are welcomed. Visit lecture halls, libraries, research labs, entrepreneur incubators, and so much more. All tour requests must go through the online booking system. Visit www.harvard.edu/visit/tours to book a visit.

A gateway into the prestigious Harvard University

TAKE IT

Take a ride or a jog along the **Charles River** *and the* **Emerald Necklace**

Along the Charles River is a beautiful urban trail designed for recreation and commuting. The waterfront views are a spectacular escape, yet in the heart of the city. Footbridges cross over the busy traffic into the famed Commonwealth Avenue Parkway. The affluent neighborhoods along the promenade are fun to explore without having to navigate with cars on the road. Boston's trail system is lined with trees, prominent statues, and windy riverways. Start from Lederman Park and end at Jamaica Pond, roughly a 7-mile stretch, to experience why Boston has always been rated one of the healthiest cities in America. Jamaica Pond is part of the Emerald Necklace, a series of linked parks that were designed by prominent landscape architect Frederick Law Olmsted.

Take yourself out to a ballgame at a ballpark that is one of the great symbols of America's favorite pastime. Nestled slightly outside downtown Boston sits **Fenway Park**, Major League Baseball's oldest ballpark—and one of the most iconic. It's where generations of fans have gone to see the Red Sox play for over a century, and you'll find locals sporting gear throughout the city. This Boston staple retains many of the same characteristics as it did when it opened in 1912. There are no nosebleed seats here; the stands are gradually sloped compared to

modern stadiums. The Boston Red Sox are one of the most prideful and accomplished franchises in all sports. Watch a game or take a tour that gives an in-depth history of the stadium and the franchise.

CHAPTER 6

PLYMOUTH, MASSACHUSETTS

This small town along Plymouth Harbor carries one of the nation's most famous names. Plymouth is home to the arrival of the *Mayflower* ship at Plymouth Rock, and the universal theme of colonists and pilgrims permeates throughout town. You might think that the notable Plymouth Rock resembles the cliff-like logo of Prudential Financial,

but it's an actual boulder of a rock. In 1620, roughly one hundred *Mayflower* Pilgrims disembarked from the shallop onto land at Plymouth Rock. For centuries, this American symbol of religious freedom and civil liberty has drawn over a million visitors per year to this city, continuing to spark the spirit of immigration, survival, and optimism.

☼ THE STORY OF PLYMOUTH ROCK

In the November 24, 2016, edition of *Scientific American*, geologist Dana Hunter wrote an article titled "The Real Story of Plymouth Rock." In it, Hunter explained:

> Plymouth Rock is made of Dedham Granite, a granodiorite that began life around 630 million years ago as part of Gondwana. It traveled with Gondwana to become part of the supercontinent of Pangea, rather like the Pilgrims first living in Leiden, Netherlands, before coming to America.

Plymouth Rock found itself on the American side of the great rift when Pangea split apart and the Atlantic Ocean was born. You cannot say it crossed an ocean, exactly, as the ocean didn't exist, but it certainly got to watch the Atlantic form. Like the Pilgrims, it initially spent its time in another part of the continent before landing at Plymouth.

Plymouth Rock is a glacial erratic. Twenty thousand years ago, it was plucked up by the great glaciers that covered huge bits of North America, rafted considerable distances, and then deposited on a coast where human history would be made a long time later. You can see pieces of this rock in many places in New England. The portion of the glacial erratic left behind at Plymouth became the famous rock it is today.

200 million years ago: Glacial erratic rock lands on shore after traveling for 400 million years.

12,000 years ago: Pokanoket tribe of Wampanoag Nation settles, calling the area Patuxet. The tribe abandons the settlement in 1616 CE after a plague kills many.

1620 CE: *Mayflower* Pilgrims arrive to find abandoned land, now renamed Plymouth on a map they were carrying, published by explorer John Smith.

The enclosed structure at Plymouth Rock. *Courtesy of See Plymouth*

TAKE IT

Save the whales with **Whale & Dolphin Conservation—**
7 Nelson Street

Plymouth offers a collection of maritime activities, such as kayaking, pirate cruises, and whale watching. But why stop at whale watching when you can get involved in the efforts to save these precious marine animals?

We still know relatively little about many whale species. Some have been identified only from bones and live in the deepest and most remote places in the ocean. Only by finding out more about their lives can we develop meaningful conservation measures that will protect them and their homes. Spend a few hours at the North American office of Whale & Dolphin Conservation and learn from policy managers and the public education coordinator about ways of doing your part to save the whales. They offer volunteer experiences on-site.

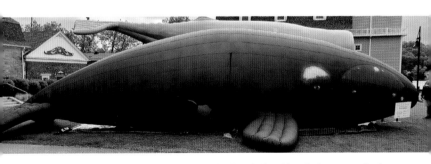

A giant inflatable whale graces the lawn of Whale & Dolphin Conservation.

INTERVIEW WITH WHALE & DOLPHIN CONSERVATION DEPUTY DIRECTOR MELISSA WALKER

What do you do?

I work on policy and educational programing. Just as with any conservation group, we must fight to protect our public lands, waters, wildlife, and engaged species. Educating the public is a large part of our organization, and in this region of the country, there are around thirty responsible whale-watching programs. Since this area is heavily trafficked, this has become our North American headquarters.

You can find us easily, since there's a huge inflatable whale outside our offices. Besides administrative duties, I also run a first-responders program, where our marine biologists are dispatched to animals in distress. Much of the public has no understanding of treating a whale or dolphin that's lying on the beach, so we heavily rely on them to contact us when an event like this takes place.

How can others get involved?

We have a program called Whale SENSE, considering there are many whale watch businesses that have to be whale sensible. SENSE stands for: **S**tick to whale-watching guidelines. **E**ducate passengers and crew. **N**otify officials of whales in trouble. **S**et an example for other boaters. **E**ncourage ocean stewardship.

Anything can help us protect whales, through cleaning up trash on the shores, outreach events, advocating to beachgoers and fisherman about their role in taking care of the habitat, and teaching people what to do when they see a whale or dolphin in distress. We have around a dozen a month that wash onto shore, and we need to study how and why.

What's your passion for this work?

My passion is for the gardeners of the ocean. I want to continue funding research to understand how important whales are to the ecosystems.

⊙ WHILE YOU'RE HERE

The city of Plymouth proves that sometimes it's OK to live in the past. Actually, the city thrives on its past, so before leaving Plymouth, make sure to see **the Plimoth Patuxet Museums**, 137 Warren Avenue, which bring to life the history of Plymouth Colony and the Indigenous homeland. Major exhibits include the Historic Patuxet Homesite, the 17th-Century English Village, the *Mayflower II*, and the Plimoth Grist Mill. This site allows you to take an authentic step back in time and learn about the ways of life back in the 1600s with many costumed interpreters who reenact daily living.

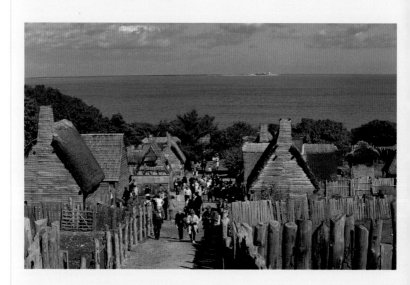

Plimoth Patuxet Museums.
Courtesy of Tricia Ellis

A replica of the *Mayflower* ship.
Courtesy of See Plymouth

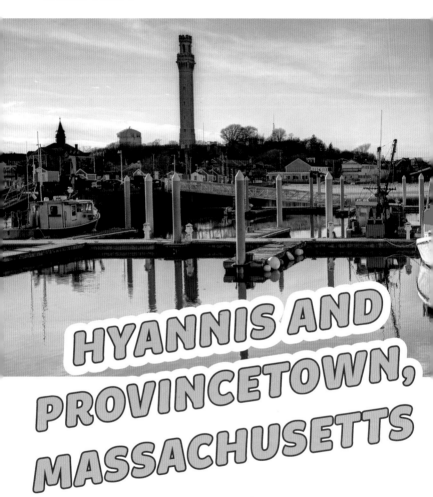

CHAPTER 7

HYANNIS AND PROVINCETOWN, MASSACHUSETTS

Decorated with a vibrant color palette and bringing cheer to visitors and residents, Hyannis has been an active Cape Cod village for generations. If Hyannis sounds familiar, it's likely due to the Kennedy family having a compound based here, and it is home to the iconic John F. Kennedy Hyannis Museum. To experience the entirety of the Cape, allow an hour to drive each way to Provincetown, which has become an LGBTQ+ favorite destination. It has the same architectural wonder as the rest of the towns on the Cape but with much more colorful flair.

Explore the Cape

In Hyannis, Main Street is truly the heart of the town and makes for a perfect stroll that offers boutique shops and local cuisine. Cape Cod is an escape for millions each year, and residents must feel like they're always on vacation. The quaint village-like towns cater to tourists, offering laidback fun with historic charm. Hyannis's Lewis Bay is where you can take a short ferry ride to Nantucket and Martha's Vineyard.

After you explore Hyannis, another reason to continue on to Provincetown to visit the tip of the Cape is that it was the site of the *Mayflower*'s first landing in the New World in 1620. The ship's occupants first came ashore on what is now Provincetown before continuing on to Plymouth, where they settled. Nearly a year later, they celebrated Thanksgiving, an event we still commemorate each November. Now, you'll find the Pilgrim Monument erected high into the sky. Centered right in the middle of town, this 252-foot feature is where President Theodore Roosevelt laid the cornerstone on August 20, 1907, and President William H. Taft led the dedication ceremony after the Pilgrim Monument's completion on August 5, 1910.

So, if you're a history buff or a nightlife enthusiast (or both!), then a trip to P-town is definitely worth the detour.

Bustling summers on Main Street in Hyannis. *Courtesy of Mary Myrick*

MAKE IT

Expand your artistic horizons with **Cape Cod School of Art**—
207 Good Templar Place, Provincetown

Provincetown is America's oldest continuous art colony mixed with a flourishing contemporary art scene. It's home to many art galleries, studios, and museums. The Cape Cod School of Art was the first school to teach outdoor figure painting.

The rich artistic history started in 1915, when Charles Hawthorne, a famous American portraitist, arrived in Provincetown for the summer. By 1916, Provincetown would grow into one of the largest art colonies in the world, attracting luminaries such as Childe Hassam, William Paxton, and Ernest Lawson.

The Provincetown Art Association and Museum (PAAM) might describe the arts legacy in Provincetown best:

> Provincetown has welcomed, nurtured and inspired artists . . . not just to create, but to connect with the town and its people. . . . Life in Provincetown has for the past 100+ years been charted by the interactions between these two groups—from destitute artists trading paintings for lodging . . . to fisherman offering a share of their day's catch to provide a meal for an artist who might otherwise go without, to the walls of local cafes and homes lined with artwork given in exchange for simple kindnesses.

Pick up some brushes and try your painting skills by drawing inspiration from one of the area's symbols, whether the Pilgrim Monument, the *Mayflower* ship, or the illustrious and colorful downtown strip. Schedule a group lesson on the beach with one of the Cape Cod School of Art's many instructors to help create your piece of Cape Cod by contacting 617-717-9568 or email capeschoolprovincetown@gmail.com.

Art on the beach, with class instruction through the Cape Art School. *Courtesy of Lori Byrne*

Iconic Architecture

You might notice that Cape Cod has a distinct trait when it comes to homes and commercial buildings. Even national franchises such as Dunkin' Donuts have to fall in line by meeting architectural designs, using this iconic theme of horizontal wood panels, white trimmings, and a worn-out wooden-roof appearance. You'd think that the many roundabouts or rotary circles in the region would steal the local flavor, but the architecture and building materials are uniquely branded as "Cape Cod architecture" and have innate coastal appeal. When you see properties on the Cape and island, the appearance will make you scream "summer."

Then you also have another very popular style in the United States, the colonial style, which originated in New England and features high-pitched, dormered roofs and two to three stories. There are one or two very large chimneys, narrow siding or brick facades, and an elaborate front entry with a portico supported by columns. The window shutters are the staple of the design. One-story wings can flank the main structure, in keeping with the symmetry. Bedrooms are on the second floor. The original colonials were very simple, lacking detail and living area; the more modern versions are more elaborate in detail and more expansive, and they feature molding along the entryway and roof eave.

A Cape Cod home.
Courtesy of Ken Wiedemann

WHAT IS CAPE COD ARCHITECTURE?

Ubiquitous to the region and much of the United States, Cape Cod–style architecture was originated by seventeenth-century English colonists, who adapted English half-timber hall-and-parlor houses to suit the bitter New England climate, creating a boxier, lower-slung silhouette to stand up to the elements. These homes often feature one and a half stories with steeply pitched or gabled roofs and one chimney on the end of the home. Dormers are now typically part of the design to extend the living area, but originally these homes were a single story. The siding is generally clapboard or wood shingles, sometimes brick. The front door is centered, typically without architectural décor, but modern versions can have a porch or portico added to the design as well as modern asymmetrical features. The floor plan is anchored by a center hall running the width of the home.

Here are a few traits that make a Cape Cod home:

- Basic rectangular shape
- One story plus a half-story second floor
- Steeply pitched roof
- Central chimney
- Center door
- Low ceilings
- Shutter-clad and dormer windows
- Cottage-like landscaping

And the materials often used:

- Oak and pine wood post-and-beam framing
- Oak and pine wood flooring
- Brick fireplaces
- Clapboard or cedar shake roof and side shingles left unpainted to weather in the elements, as seen in original Cape Cod cottages
- Cape Cod–style exteriors were painted white with black shutters, which became a classic color combination starting with the revival of the mid-twentieth century, but today, other color combinations are common.

Ahoy, Matey!

On your drive between Hyannis and Provincetown, you can experience Cape Cod's newest interactive science museum featuring real pirates and treasures. **Whydah Pirate Museum** at 674 Route 28 in West Yarmouth has become a must-see attraction that touches on local history. Visitors can interact with the world's only authenticated pirate treasure, discovered in 1984 off the coast of Wellfleet.

The *Whydah* was a fully rigged galley ship built by the British to travel between Africa, the Caribbean, and Great Britain. During one of its voyages in 1717, it was captured by the famed pirate Samuel "Black Sam" Bellamy. Over the following year, the *Whydah* and its crew pirated fifty-three vessels, collecting their riches and treasures.

During an infamous storm off the coast of Wellfleet, the *Whydah* ship sunk in 1717; there were only two survivors. The *Whydah*'s legend was passed down among generations throughout the Cape, since its treasure laid just 500 feet offshore for over 250 years.

Provincetown resident Barry Clifford dedicated years to the discovery of the *Whydah*'s real pirate treasure, eventually unearthing it. For the first time ever, it is now on display for Cape residents and tourists to see.

TAKE IT

Continue your journey in true nautical fashion with the
Steamship Authority

Take the Steamship Authority to Nantucket, which is 26 miles from Cape Cod's mainland port of Hyannis, which is located at 69 South Street. You can either take a leisurely two-hour-and-fifteen-minute voyage on the Steamship Authority's traditional ferries or ride in style and luxury on board its seasonal high-speed passenger-only ferry, the *MV Iyanough*, which gets you to Nantucket in just one hour. The other provider to consider is Hy-Line Cruises, which also runs year-round.

CHAPTER 8

NANTUCKET, MASSACHUSETTS

In Nantucket, beaches are all around, and the pre–Civil War architecture of quant cottages and federal-style homes lines cobblestone roads. These sights and Nantucket's bustling whaling industry have inspired some of America's greatest literary classics—and some poetry. Nantucket's name has inspired numerous limericks. One of the earliest, written by Professor Dayton Vorhees in 1902, has become very well known:

There once was a man from Nantucket
Who kept all his cash in a bucket.
But his daughter, named Nan,
Ran away with a man
And as for the bucket, Nantucket.

The Nantucket Hotel & Resort—
77 Easton Street

Treat yourself in this historic hotel that has been dazzling guests since 1891. The resort is a perfect representation of Nantucket's tradition and class, and you'll be treated like royalty with a gracious staff, elegant dining, and breathtaking rooms. The property is steps away from the cobblestone streets of downtown and Nantucket's iconic beaches. This year-round hotel takes you into a world of sea life, through nautical-themed decor and a colorful ocean palette. It alludes to the ocean air, the sea breezes, the dunes, and the sand.

This aerial scene of Nantucket shows the enormous hotel in the heart of town. *Courtesy of the Nantucket Hotel & Resort*

THE STORY OF *MOBY-DICK*

As told by Nantucket Historical Association:

Herman Melville wrote his classic novel *Moby-Dick* (1851) without having visited the island of Nantucket. The island and its whaling history form the backbone of his novel, and indeed are central symbols in the epic journey of the *Pequod* in its hunt for Moby-Dick, the white whale. Melville based the essentials of his plot, and the final climactic ramming of the *Pequod*, upon all that he had read about Nantucket's whaling industry, and in particular, the gruesome tale of the Nantucket whaleship *Essex*. After the publication of *Moby-Dick*, Melville finally visited the island, and met face-to-face with Captain George Pollard Jr., the captain who survived one of the most harrowing ordeals at sea in human history.

Nantucket Historical Association and the Whaling Museum. *Courtesy of Bill Hoenk Photography*

Nantucket's Whaling Legacy

Learn about how the island became the whaling capital at one time at the **Nantucket Whaling Museum**, 13 Broad Street. The Whaling Museum is part of the Nantucket Historical Association (NHA), which is the world's most comprehensive resource and principal steward of Nantucket history. The museum tells the inspiring stories of the island through its collections, programs, and properties. The NHA's vast holdings contain thousands of paintings, prints and drawings, baskets, lighting devices, scrimshaw artworks, whaling tools and implements, pieces of furniture and decorative arts, and historic properties and sites—plus the complete skeleton of a 47-foot sperm whale. This self-guided museum shares what it was like to be aboard a ship in the nineteenth century, hunting whales with harpoons. Also explored is the history of how Nantucket became the hotspot of the whaling industry. Tour the Hadwen & Barney Oil and Candle Factory and learn about the lucrative trade of oil and candle production. If you didn't know anything about the industry before visiting, you'll certainly leave with a much more thorough understanding.

An exhibit at Nantucket Historical
Association and the Whaling Museum.
Courtesy of Bill Hoenk Photography

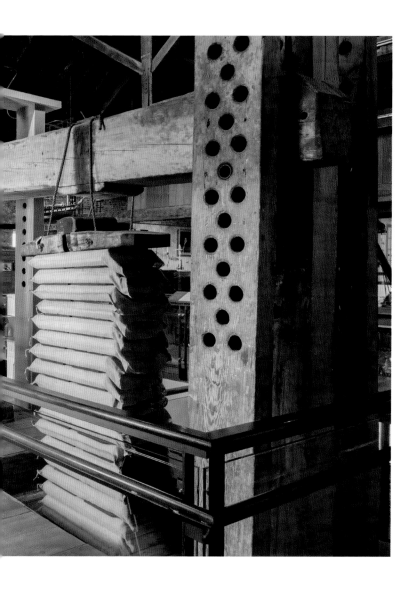

MAKE IT

Create Nantucket baskets with **Whale Tail Weaving**— *23 Old South Wharf*

Don't expect to take a whale home with you, but the next best option is to handcraft a piece of old whalesmanship. In the early to mid-1800s, whaling expeditions took sailors on clipper ships offshore for years. These hunters had to be courageous, adventurous, and hyperalert, but there were times that left them bored. Sailors would spend their free time carving whalebones and weaving baskets. These baskets were made for purely utilitarian purposes, but when the sailors docked in Nantucket, the baskets often became cherished as family heirlooms that would be passed through generations. Nowadays, many tourists seek out these baskets as a piece of the industry's history, and Whale Tail Weaving provides the opportunity to make one of your own. Contact Bridget Wiatrowski at bridget@whaletailweaving.com or visit www.whaletailweaving.com to schedule an appointment. Expect a two-hour-long lesson on handcrafting accessories, such as bracelets and earrings, in the same way that baskets are made.

Bridget Wiatrowski demonstrates the art of basket weaving. *Courtesy of Bridget Wiatrowski*

INTERVIEW WITH WEAVER BRIDGET WIATROWSKI

What was your inspiration for Whale Tail Weaving?

I'm originally from Cape Cod year-round. I say year-round because when I was a kid, the Cape was a seasonal destination. My parents enrolled me into sailing classes because the waters were so accessible to our home. I cherished the ocean, like many of us locals do, and got into racing sailboats. I continued racing through college. My parents weren't sailors, but my mother was into weaving and fashion. She wanted to continue this dying art of basket weaving that was so prominent to our culture from the whaling industry. Every week, especially throughout Cape Cod winters, my mom would gather up her supplies and visit her "Basket Ladies." These Basket Lady sessions intrigued me, but it wasn't until much later that I learned to weave myself. I now have a sense of how important that activity was to her—socially, as well as for the satisfaction and joy of creating something beautiful with your own hands and keeping a dying art alive.

What are your thoughts on the whaling industry?

Well, it doesn't exist in America any longer. We have many whale and dolphin conservations in this area. The only countries that are still active are Norway, Japan, and Iceland. The whale industry literally lit the world, but the whale population was severely depleted from being overfished. In the 1800s, whale oil was this region's form of lighting and lubrication. In school, we learned about the history of whaling and thought of old captains like folk heroes. We used to take field trips to the homes of captains on the Cape and islands. This area was very seasonal, from the fishing and the tourism industry, so we grew up appreciating and respecting the history of whale hunting.

Why was Nantucket the Whaling Capital of the World?

The waters are deep, and Nantucket had a perfect harbor. Not to mention, the spirit and character of the men was adventurous. America was using floating ships like lighthouses to prevent shipwrecks caused by shoals, sandbars, and weather. The weathers of New England were prone to ever-changing conditions, so they invented these lightships that acted as mobile navigation stations. These ships didn't have sails; rather, big masts. There were crews for these ships and the clipper hunting ships, and Nantucket became the hub.

What are the traditions you're trying to keep alive?

People are all about the baskets that were often sold by sailors in town. They were even decorated with carved whale teeth, known as scrimshaw art. I wanted to keep this art form and demand alive, so I learned from my mother how to weave these baskets, using maple wood and rattan. I remember my mother steaming long blades, so she could create the baskets in the kitchen. I wanted to make a line of accessories, so it wasn't just limited to baskets. It used to be a fashion statement for affluent women to carry around handcrafted purses made of rattan and wood. These items are not cheap.

On a sidenote, my husband and I started a nonprofit to make the waters more accessible to everyone. Growing up on the Cape and around the islands, there were limited public waters. Sailing and boating is not the most accessible sport—there's only so many places to dock your boat. It's true that nobody owns the ocean, but getting to it is difficult. We are trying to support community-boating efforts. We anticipate supporting Sea Scouts and other community programs in order to increase participation in on-the-water education. Visit lbay.org for more information.

Opposite: Customers get hooked, just like the fish (*left*). Showcasing the size of the tuna (*right*). *Courtesy of Carl Bois*

TAKE IT

Learn to sportfish with **Topspin Fishing—**
34 Washington Street

Ever gone fishing for tuna? This two-and-a-half-hour trip is perfect for people who want to try out some sportfishing but don't want to be on the water all day. Typically, Topspin Fishing fishes at Great Point, which offers fantastic bluefishing. The bluefish are aggressive, strong, and a blast to catch. If you've never been fishing, you'll get hooked. Occasionally, striped bass, bluefish, fluke, black seabass, bonito, and false albacore are also fished, depending on the time of year. Captain Carl Bois guarantees you'll have success catching a tuna, and as the locals say, "It's wicked fun." He'll take you and five others out on his 35-foot boat, which can handle some of Nantucket's roughest shallow rips. Book a trip by calling 508-246-6210 or emailing Topspinack@gmail.com.

CHAPTER 9

MARTHA'S VINEYARD, MASSACHUSETTS

After your visit to Nantucket, take the Hy-line Cruises ferry to Martha's Vineyard to find out why presidents of the United States often schedule vacations to this pristine island destination spewing of merit. Martha's Vineyard is treated as if it were someone's personal estate, since the island is well manicured and maintained. Distinction is bursting from the soft sandy beaches, the neighborhood front porches, and the harbor. Just in one season, the

population of the island grows from 17,000 to 200,000, because this destination is like an enormous wedding venue. Contrary to its name, there are no vineyards on Martha's Vineyard, but it is believed that there were wild grapevines all over the island when it was first settled. The Vineyard is the ultimate destination—even if you still have nightmares from the classic *Jaws* scenes from the iconic movie series filmed on the island.

Sunrise at Edgartown Lighthouse
Courtesy of Peter Simon

HOW DID MARTHA'S VINEYARD GET ITS NAME?

As explained by Rebecca Beatrice Brooks of History of Massachusetts Blog:

The answer has been lost to time but some sources claim that the island was named after an early Massachusetts explorer's infant daughter or wife.

The Wampanoag natives who originally lived on the island called it by two names: Noepe, meaning "land between the streams," and Capawack.

In 1524, when Italian explorer Giovanni da Verrazzano visited New England he explored the waters around Cape Cod and named the island Luisa.

Many years later, in 1602, English explorer Bartholomew Gosnold embarked on an expedition to the East Coast during which he mapped and named many of the locations he saw, particularly Cape Cod.

During the expedition, Gosnold explored the Nantucket Sound and the waters around Martha's Vineyard. There he observed a series of islands, including a small uninhabited island known as No-Man's Land and another larger island now known as Martha's Vineyard.

Some sources say that Gosnold decided to give No-Man's Land the name Martha's Vineyard, either after his daughter, Martha, who had died as an infant in 1598, or after his mother-in-law Martha Golding, who helped finance the expedition.

They also say that Gosnold gave the larger island the name Martin's Vineyard, possibly after Gosnold's shipmate, Captain John Martin.

One of the men onboard, Gabriel Archer, wrote an account of the expedition, later published in 1625, during which he described finding and naming No-Man's Land: "From this opening the main lieth south-west, which coasting along we saw a disinhabited island, which so afterward appeared unto us: we bore with it, and named it Martha's Vineyard."

Gosnold was also responsible for giving Cape Cod its name, naming it after the abundant supply of cod fish in the waters around the cape.

Dress sharp! Martha's Vineyard is preppy, like the rest of the Cape Cod culture, so if you're searching for a new style or threads or just want to fit in, take some time to stroll along Main Street in Edgartown. I'm not someone who is into fashion, but even I was influenced to purchase a new colorful wardrobe. After you shop, grab a bite to eat at **The Wharf** at 3 Main Street, Edgartown, for the classic seafood and pub experience. Or try a raw seafood bar at **The Port Hunter**, located on 55 Main Street.

An elegant evening on the streets of Edgartown.
Courtesy of Peter Simon

Float Back to the Mainland

After your time in the Vineyard, take the ferry back to Cape Cod, either to Hyannis or Woods Hole in Falmouth. You can take your car onto the ferry, which is an experience in itself.

CHAPTER 10

Named after the Wareham in England and considered the gateway to the Cape, Wareham (pronounced "wear-em") is filled with unique local experiences, including the hub of cranberry bogs, Cape Verdean / Portuguese cultural influences, and local scrimshaw and sea-glass art. Wareham's campaign slogan is "It's Better Before the Bridges," referring to the bridges to Cape Cod. The city proudly boasts deep industrial roots, and Wareham is not the "fanciest" town around in comparison to its neighbors, but it has 57 miles of coastline, the most of any city on the Cape. You

can live on the water or in the woods, on 5 acres or on 0.25 acres in the middle of a dense neighborhood of cottages. There's cultural and socioeconomic diversity in Wareham, and people in this town are unique—many very kindhearted, down-to-earth people with a good sense of humor. An enormous number of charitable organizations are registered to the residents of Wareham. The village of Onset (in Wareham) used to be a world-famous destination back in the early 1900s, home to seaside resorts, attractions, and gambling.

TAKE IT

Harvest cranberries at **Makepeace Farms**—*146 Tihonet Road*

The world-famous cranberry juice made by Ocean Spray is contracted by Makepeace Farms. One of the most unique sights in agriculture is to gaze over a bog of floating cranberries, and if you get a chance to put waders on and go into the knee-high-deep bog, you'll feel like you're walking through a pond of freshly pressed juice. The harvesting process is not what you think. Cranberries are grown on shrubs, then the fields are floated with water, so picking them off the plant is much easier to collect with a special combine that spins and reels the sour red berries. Take a tour and get a chance to learn about a crop that Massachusetts is very proud of. Don't leave without your own bottle of cranberry juice and some dried cranberries, known as craisins.

The land of berries.
Provided by Makepeace Farms

A tour group observes the harvest of cranberries.
Courtesy of Makepeace Farms

WHAT'S THE HISTORY OF BOGGING?

As explained by Makepeace Farms:

Tens of thousands of years ago, receding glaciers carved out cavities in the land that evolved into cranberry bogs. Newly formed kettle ponds filled with sand, clay, and debris formed the perfect environment for vines to spread across the South Shore, Cape Cod, Martha's Vineyard, and Nantucket. Massachusetts was born with cranberry bogs. For two hundred years, it has been where tradition has met innovation.

Wampanoag People across southeastern Massachusetts have enjoyed the annual harvest of *sasumuneash* (wild cranberries) for 12,000 years. Some ate berries fresh while others dried them to make *nasampe* (grits) or *pemmican* (a mix of berries, dried meat, and animal fat that could last for months). Medicine men, or *powwows*, used cranberries in traditional healing rituals to fight fever, swelling, and even seasickness.

Europeans exploring and settling New England in the sixteenth and seventeenth centuries were not surprised to see *sasumuneash*. Many were familiar with European cranberry varieties, which grew in the boggy regions of southern England and in the low-lying Netherlands. The English had many names for the fruit, but "craneberries" was the most common because many thought the flower resembled the head of a Sandhill crane.

Cultivation of the cranberry began in 1816, shortly after Captain Henry Hall, a Revolutionary War veteran, of Dennis, Massachusetts, noticed that the wild cranberries in his bogs grew better when sand blew over them. Captain Hall began transplanting cranberry vines and spreading sand on them. When others heard of Hall's technique, it was quickly copied. Continuing throughout the nineteenth century, the number of growers increased steadily.

While initially criticized for tinkering with vines, the idea of growing and selling cranberries commercially soon caught on, and local landowners eagerly converted their swamps, wetlands, peat swamps, and wet meadows into cranberry bogs. By 1885, Plymouth County boasted 1,347 acres under cultivation; Barnstable County had 2,408. By 1900, the number of acres tripled, making Cape Cod a household name. "Cranberry Fever" struck and the industry boomed. As late as 1927, the cranberry harvest remained so vital to local and state economies that Massachusetts children could be excused from school to work the bogs during harvest season.

Expansion fueled innovation. Growing cranberries demanded long hours of back-breaking work. Farmers eagerly sought new tools to build better bogs and harvest cranberries more efficiently. In the 1880s, wooden cranberry scoops started to replace traditional hand-picking; sorters and screening equipment soon followed. Expansion also meant new workers on the bogs. Although many growers still relied on traditional family and community support during the harvest, demands for higher wages provided opportunities for newly arrived immigrants from Finland and the Cape Verdean Islands seeking better economic opportunities and the chance at an improved life.

Expansion and increased global demand also meant the need for a system of grading and branding berries. New agricultural co-ops like the Cape Cod Cranberry Sales Company set market prices for berries and regulated distribution to ensure that growers received the fairest prices for their berries and customers got the best product.

By 1871, the first association of cranberry growers had formed and now, US farmers harvest approximately 40,000 acres of cranberries each year.

Today, the industry continues to grow and evolve to meet new demands and tastes for sweet, sour, and everything in between. Cranberry growers remain innovators—as flexible and adaptable as ever. Recent slow and local food movements rekindled interest among consumers in food origins, offering growers a chance to showcase their craft and passion with new audiences.

MAKE IT

Create nautical art with **EcHo Elizabeth & Company Home Offerings—***5 Elm Street*

Nautical art is a way of life near the Cape, and artist Elizabeth Sellon embodies the true nature and passion behind the work. In a historic company store, Elizabeth hosts individuals, mostly locals, looking to create art with her. A master at sea-glass art and scrimshaw art, she also offers tips and tools for creating art at home. All the items that Elizabeth and her students create are natural and eco-friendly products, because she understands how certain materials negatively affect the environment and horticulture. Her motive is to make functional accessories for life and apply skills to grow things and cook things. Elizabeth offers workshops with 196 local artists—and the art is as diverse as the people who make it. She says that making things with your own hands allows you to value art.

When you contact her to set up an appointment to create some nautical art, Elizabeth suggests creating a silk painting of the local landscape, using watercolors on felt fabric. This great memento of Wareham will inspire great conversation.

Watercoloring on felt. *Provided by Elizabeth Sellon*

Spend Time at the Beach

Locals can be found relaxing at **Onset Beach** (186 Onset Avenue), a popular sandy beach offering lifeguards, concessions, and restrooms, plus summertime events. Located in the Onset Bay, surrounded by coves in the greater Buzzards Bay, Onset Beach has calm waters like a lake—perfect for wading or taking out a kayak. Boat rentals can be found at the beach, along with the amenities of many restaurants and shops. The views are spectacular; you can see Wickets Island and Onset Island, many boats navigating the waters, and massive Cape Cod architecture homes.

 WHILE YOU'RE HERE

New England is known for specialized dishes that have been around for centuries, while other items have been recently integrated into the local culture. Of course, there are the iconic lobster rolls, clam chowder, Boston baked beans, and Boston cream pie, and then there's Del's lemonade, whoopie pies, fluffernutter, and coffee milk. But, for those wanting an extravagant social event, gather around for a clambake. Clambakes are scattered throughout the region and can be found by a quick search on the internet. Wareham hosts an annual event, which takes place in August and includes over 450 people and involves 46 bushels of clams.

The New England clambake is a custom that dates back well before the Pilgrims landed on Plymouth Rock. Early Native Americans cooked the region's abundant seafood, such as clams (quahogs, a clam common to the Eastern seaboard) and lobsters, by digging a pit in beach sand, using hot rocks for heat, and creating steam via wet seaweed. Along the way, other ingredients such as corn, potatoes, and onions were introduced. Clambakes didn't become social functions until the 1900s, driven most likely by romanticism and good old Yankee capitalism. Today, certain groups and communities have their own ways of doing a clambake, but the common practice is to cook by steaming the ingredients over layers of seaweed in a pit oven.

CHAPTER 11

NEWPORT, RHODE ISLAND

Rhode Island is known as the Ocean State, and there's no better representation of that moniker than its distinguished city of Newport. Founded in 1639, this "Sailing Capital of the World" delivers everything nautical from restaurants on piers to cliff walks, pristine beaches, and an ocean drive that captures seaside views. The Claiborne Pell suspension bridge inclines over Narragansett Bay,

providing grand waterscape views that will take your breath away—from observing the abundance of boats dotted across the choppy waters to a mansion set on a rock. Home to only 25,000 residents, Newport and its narrowly built roads take in a half-million visitors per year who are eager to shop, attend a concert, get in touch with history, and—of course—jump onto a sailboat.

TAKE IT

*Learn to sail with **Sail Newport**—72 Fort Adams Drive*

Starting from Brenton Cove, navigating around Goat Island in Newport Harbor and out to the Narragansett Bay, sailing in Newport is one of the most thrilling—and possibly terrifying—activities you'll do in your life. Sail Newport sailing school offers guides to take you through the nearby waters, teaching you how to use only the winds and sails to maneuver large yachts along rocky shores and through unassuming, choppy waters. Depending on the speed, you can find yourself sitting high on the edge of a sailboat that seems like it's tipping, making you look straight down into the water. And there are times where you may need to stop abruptly before crashing into other boats—and there's no gas to speed up or brakes to stop! It's quite an art to control the winds through sails, and it's a major adjustment from operating motorboats. The instructors will teach it all on a sloop-style sailboat for up to two hours. Visit www.sailnewport.org for reservations.

HOW DID NEWPORT BECOME THE SAILING CAPITAL?

As explained by 12 Meter Yachts Charters:

Newport has a longstanding sailing history that is evident everywhere in the "City-by-the-Sea," from the many colonial sea captains' homes that line the streets of Newport's downtown, to the busy Newport Harbor that is a destination and home port, to some of the most renowned sailing and motor yachts in the world. Newport even has a busy downtown street, America's Cup Avenue, dedicated to the most famous sailing race! Since the city's founding in 1639, Newporters have taken advantage of their city's seaside location by using sailing for trade, pleasure, sport, and business.

In the eighteenth century, Newport became a worldwide maritime trading center. Newport, along with Boston, New York, Philadelphia, and Charleston, emerged as one of the five leading ports in colonial North America. Although Newport is significantly smaller in size and population than those other cities. Economic growth created by maritime trade generated an expansion of Newport's harbor and downtown. Over 150 wharves were built, and sailing cargo ships crowded Newport Harbor. Many of Newport's famous landmarks were built during this time, including Trinity Church, the Redwood Library, and the Brick Market.

In the nineteenth century, the United States Navy officially sailed into Newport and became a major part of Newport's economy. During the Civil War, the US Naval Academy was temporarily moved to Newport. The USS *Constitution* and the *America*, the first America's Cup winner, were sailing in Newport and were used for midshipmen training while the US Naval Academy was located in Newport.

Sailing in Newport Harbor.
Courtesy of Discover Newport

After the Civil War, the Naval Academy was moved back to Annapolis, but the Navy stayed in Newport. During this time, the first naval laboratory for torpedo testing was built in Newport Harbor on Goat Island; the Naval Training Station and Naval War College were also established in Newport. Later, Newport and Narragansett Bay were used as a major port for US Navy ships. At one time, more than a quarter of the US Navy's Atlantic Fleet was stationed in Newport. Today, although Newport is not a home port to the Navy's ships, there is a retired aircraft carrier at the base. With the Naval War College and other training facilities still in Newport, the Navy continues to be an important part of Newport's economy.

Later in the nineteenth century, Newport Harbor went from being a maritime trading center to a sailing playground for the rich and famous. During this time, many of America's most influential businessmen, with names like Vanderbilt, Astor, Belmont, and Berwind, built summer homes in Newport. With this influx of wealth, Newport Harbor became a major yachting destination. The Vanderbilts, the Astors, the Manvilles, J. P. Morgan, and many others brought their luxurious sailing yachts to Newport. In 1883, Newport came into the sailing spotlight when the New York Yacht Club (NYYC) held its first annual regatta there. Newport was also added as a stop on the NYYC annual cruise from New York to New England. As the interest in Newport sailing grew, two local yacht clubs were formed: the Newport Yacht Club in 1893 and the Ida Lewis Yacht Club in 1928. The NYYC also officially came to Newport and formed Station #9, a Newport clubhouse, for its yachting events. The Newport NYYC clubhouse has been the center of an impressive number of international sailing events, including America's Cup sailing defenses, the Annapolis to Newport race, and the World Championships of the One Ton Ocean Racers.

For over fifty years of the twentieth century, the most coveted sailing race in the world—the America's Cup—was held in Newport. Since the first America's Cup defense in 1870, the NYYC held the America's Cup races in New York. However, in the 1930s after an increased interest in sailing in the "City-by-the-Sea," the NYYC brought the America's Cup sailing races to Newport. During the 1930s, the spectacular J-Boats raced for the America's Cup. At over 100 feet long and with a crew of over twenty men, the building and sailing of these yachts was a very expensive endeavor. Some of Newport's most wealthy summertime residents were very active in America's Cup sailing, including Harold Vanderbilt, who funded campaigns and sailed in the 1930, 1934, and 1937 America's Cup events.

After a halt in America's Cup sailing because of war, the 12-meter yachts brought a new era of America's Cup racing to Newport starting in 1958 and continuing to 1983, when, for the first time in over 130 years, the America's Cup was lost by the NYYC and won by Australia.

Sailing remains a tradition in Newport to this day. Narragansett Bay and Newport Harbor are busier than ever with large and small sailing boats. Major sailing regattas are started, finished, and held in Newport. The Newport to Bermuda sailing race starts in Newport biennially in June. Single-handed races, trans-Atlantic, and round-the-world races use Newport as a starting and finishing port. Sailing tours, team-building races, and charter sails are major attractions for Newport's corporate and private visitors.

🏨 CHECKING IN

The Chanler at Cliff Walk—
117 Memorial Boulevard

This luxury hotel exemplifies Gilded Age elegance, and its property is housed along the famed Cliff Walk and overlooks Newport's beaches. The hotel offers twenty distinctive rooms that are elegantly decorated to evoke different time periods. The Chandler is the ultimate hotel experience, including a five-star restaurant, outdoor dining on the manicured private oasis filled with gardens and serene views, and gracious hospitality. This will be one of the most memorable hotel stays in your lifetime, since it represents quintessential Newport—which means excellence.

A special touch from gracious staff at The Chanler. *Courtesy of The Chanler*

Set for a fairy-tale stay at The Chanler.
Courtesy of The Chanler

Take a Deep Dive into Sailing History

To learn more about sailing and Newport, visit the **Sailing Museum and the National Sailing Hall of Fame** at 365 Thames Street. As the museum explains, "Water is essential for all life, but among sailors it's also essential for living. The Sailing Museum is America's home port, celebrating the mythic bond of those who go down to the sea for inner revival, athletic competition, or simple soul-nourishing pleasure."

When you enter the museum, you're prompted to select from one of seven boats to tailor your museum adventure. Collect virtual rewards as you complete activities, design a boat, or create your own burgee and take it home with you. If you want to experience what it's like to compete, there are high-tech exhibits with built-in "stealth learning" opportunities that share the ins and outs of the sport, challenging you to build your skills and teamwork. Experience what it's like to fly over the water with SailGP in the immersive film dome, or test your strength against the pros on the grinders.

It is said that sailing is the oldest sport in competition; predating the modern Olympics, the America's Cup has fueled design, innovation, and pure athleticism since 1851. Get to know the legends who shaped the sport, test your knowledge, and revel in one of sailing's many great moments.

Walk along the Waves

Walk the nearby **Cliff Walk** for a stunning panoramic view of the ocean, with waves crashing against the jagged rocks on one side and century-old Gilded Age mansions on the other. The trail is 3.5 miles, but you can turn around at any time.

A walkway designed to allow people
to step alongside the crashing waves.
Courtesy of Discover Newport

Newport's Cliff Walk serves up breathtaking views. *Courtesy of Discover Newport*

Also popular with tourists are Newport's mansion tours. During the Gilded Age, America's wealthiest families flocked to the "City-by-the-Sea" and its surrounding areas, making Newport their summertime playground. The meticulous preservation of more than a dozen of these homes gives us intimate access to the artistry, personality, and complex culture that went into these colossal time capsules. All that being said, simply having access to and enjoying the breathtaking grounds and cliffside vantage points of these homes is a treasure to cherish. The most popular are the Breakers, Rosecliff, Marble House, the Elms, and Chateau-sur-Mer. Go on a self-guided tour or stop by the Visitors Center to book a bus tour. The hours are 10 a.m. to 4 p.m.

The Breakers estate dazzles inside and out. *Courtesy of Discover Newport*

WHAT WAS THE GILDED AGE?

Between 1870 and the late 1890s, American entrepreneurs emerged as tycoons because of the Industrial Revolution. The period of unprecedented growth of industry, transportation, and technology prospered. It was also a time of economic devastation and dangerous working conditions for labor. The likes of the Vanderbilts, du Ponts, Rockefellers, Astors, Carnegies, Goulds, Morgans, Dukes, Roosevelts, Whitneys, and Hearsts all acquired enormous wealth, and their influence still lives on today. "The Gilded Age" had become known as the period of greedy, corrupt industrialists, bankers, and politicians. Inspired by the disparities between the elite and the working class, Mark Twain wrote a classic satirical novel called *The Gilded Age: A Tale of Today*.

Among the lasting vestiges of the Gilded Age are a number of estates built during the era by these wealthy families. There is nothing quite like the homes built during this period, where American "royalty" was shamelessly displayed. These weren't just homes, but also estates boasting extraordinary elitism, where the wealthy impressed the wealthy. The quality of the architecture, intricate touches, and materials still shines today. One of the most famous is Biltmore, which is located in Asheville, North Carolina, and was the family estate of George and Edith Vanderbilt. Construction started on the 250-room chateau in 1889, prior to the couple's marriage, and continued for six years. The home had thirty-five bedrooms, forty-three bathrooms, sixty-five fireplaces, a dairy, a horse barn, and beautiful formal and informal gardens.

Another Vanderbilt mansion is **the Breakers** in Newport, Rhode Island. The summer home of railroad mogul Cornelius Vanderbilt, the Italian Renaissance–style home has seventy rooms, a stable, and a carriage house.

Rosecliff, also in Newport, was completed in 1902. The oceanfront home was contracted by Theresa Fair Oelrichs and built to resemble the Grand Trianon of Versailles. Today, it's best known as the backdrop for movie scenes in *The Great Gatsby*, *High Society*, *27 Dresses*, and *True Lies*.

MAKE IT

Cook up a favorite New England dish with **Newport Chowder Company**—*food trucks around Newport*

The most iconic dish of New England might be lobster, but clam chowder takes a close second. Learn how to make Rhode Island's version of New England seafood chowder from an award-winning chowder recipe by Katie Potter. It all started with Katie's mother, Muriel Barclay de Tolly, who was born in Nova Scotia, Canada, and immigrated to the United States with her husband, George.

In 1985, she opened the famous Muriel's restaurant in Newport with the help of her six children.

On a dare, she entered her seafood chowder in the Newport Chowder Festival and went on to win the contest for three consecutive years. This placed her in the Newport, Rhode Island, Chowder Hall of Fame in 1989. Although she retired from her restaurant in 1999, her delicious seafood chowder recipe, with its secret spices, is still available. The legacy has been passed on to Katie, who runs two food trucks and a cart around the city of Newport, and they are bustling during the summer months.

Katie is offering instruction on how she makes the award-winning chowder. Schedule an appointment two weeks in advance by emailing Newportchowdercompany@gmail.com or calling 401-447-8373. Her recipes are also available on the website (www.newportchowdercompany.com), but take the opportunity to cook side by side with a local cooking legend.

Ready to serve. *Courtesy of Katie Potter*

MAKE IT

Create iconic art with **Scrimshanders**—*14 Bowen's Wharf*

Scrimshaw art was a pastime developed by whalemen to pass the time while on whale-hunting voyages. Because the time between kills could sometimes stretch a month or longer, sailors starting engraving and carving whalebone and whale teeth. This became an American folk art, which dates back to the nineteenth century. The art is scarce and sacred, because the whaling industry no longer exists the way it once did. The art continues on, using ivory dating back hundreds of years, and you can learn more about it through classes offered by Scrimshanders. The founder, Brian Kiracofe, has been engraving nautical scenes on ancient walrus, prehistoric mammoth, and recycled piano key ivory for over forty years, specializing in Newport scenes and custom designs. Classes are offered for a fee per person and last up to ninety minutes.

"I will explain the history of the art of scrimshaw from early whaling to modern," relates Brian. "I explain the materials used and the laws governing the materials. Guests will be shown examples of all materials, such as whale teeth and woolly mammoth ivory, as well as several 19c original sailor-made artifacts, such as a whalebone fid, a clothespin, and sailmakers seam rubber."

Brian will also lead guests on a studio tour of his workspace, where he will show guests how to prepare materials for engraving. "We will sand and polish an antique piano key ivory so it is ready to engrave," he says. "Afterward, I will demonstrate the art of engraving step by step before instructing guests on how to make their own piece of scrimshaw." Participants will leave with a finished piece along with a small bag of ancient mammoth ivory, a scribe, and ink to continue creating scrimshaw at home.

Scrimshaw art has deep ties to the New England region, and although the whaling industry is a touchy subject, its product is highly valuable. Most of the art for sale is over a thousand dollars. Whalebone and whale teeth are considered antiques and are not allowed to be sold outside the state. Documentation of its origin is strictly required.

Scrimshaw art on whale teeth. *Courtesy of Brian Kiracofe*

CHAPTER 12

MYSTIC, CONNECTICUT

Modern day meets yesteryear in Mystic. Boats are a part of the town's landscape, where glamorous yachts share the Mystic River and Mystic Harbor waters with enormous wooden whaling fleets. Church steeples line the skies, the Bascule drawbridge salutes the town's rich maritime past, and the colonial-era sea captains' homes bring

distinction. Mystic is not actually a legally recognized town; instead, it's a village within Groton and Stonington. This village covering 4 square miles was settled in 1654, as a shipbuilding seaport village and a safe harbor for tall ships to weather a storm. It's now Connecticut's tourist gem, with easy access to anyone driving Interstate 95.

MAKE IT

Keep a traditional craft alive at **Mystic Knotwork**—
2 Holmes Street or 25 Cottrell Street

Keeping the nautical knotwork tradition alive is at the center of Mystic Knotwork's mission. Tributing the sailors, this "Made in America" small business understands that every serious home decorator knows that knots are part of that nautical look. Even the humble sailor bracelet can be a means to touch a past that stretches back centuries.

Visitors have the opportunity to learn knot art, which first means learning how to tie knots. Many techniques include the reef knot, sheet bend, figure eight, bowline, clove hitch, and cleat hitch. The terms may sound foreign, but sailors used these knot-tying techniques every day and mastered the craft on long voyages at sea.

Mystic Knotwork is the first and oldest knot shop in the United States, where artisans from around the world learned knot tying that popularized the decorative pieces for coastal villages. Inside the workshop of a 180-year-old building, you have a chance to create your own sailor bracelet or other accessories such as napkin rings and coasters. Arrange to take a twenty-minute lesson from one of their shopworkers by calling Sue Waterman at 401-743-2149 or emailing suew@mysticknotwork.com.

Sailor knotwork bracelets.
Courtesy of Sue Waterman

The Thimble Islands.
Courtesy of the Connecticut Office of Tourism

TAKE IT

Enjoy an island adventure with **Thimble Island Cruise**—
Stony Creek Dock, 4 Indian Point Road, Branford

As you head west on Interstate 95 toward New York State, it's easy to miss Connecticut's shoreline, although it's a stone's throw away. Any local would direct you to Connecticut's archipelago, called the Thimble Islands. A touch of paradise, these twenty-five small, rocky, wooded islands—some with Victorian summer cottages—are on wonderful display for boaters, kayakers, and paddlers. They were discovered by a Dutch explorer in 1614, but the colonists didn't claim land grants to occupy the islands until 1716. The islands became a great place to harvest seaweed, which was used as fertilizer for farmers; a hub for commercial fishing, including harvesting oysters; and, of course, a remote getaway. The islands are named after the thimbleberry bush, which continues to thrive today.

The *Sea Mist* cruise offers a forty-five-minute, narrated ferry ride that explores much of the island's history and present-day life of the island, which is inhabited by one hundred families. Visit thimbleislandcruise.com to book your seat.

Connect to the American Maritime Experience

The Mystic Seaport Museum is the nation's leading maritime museum. Founded in 1929 to gather and preserve the rapidly disappearing artifacts of America's seafaring past, the museum has grown to become a national center for research and education, with the mission to "inspire an enduring connection to the American maritime experience." To preserve and interpret maritime history, the museum employs an incredibly knowledgeable staff composed of scholars, librarians, historical interpreters, educators, scientists, musicians, and skilled artisans. It's truly a remarkable campus that covers 19 acres along the Mystic River. The museum is composed of a re-created New England coastal village, a working shipyard, formal exhibit halls, and state-of-the-art artifact storage facilities. You can learn about five hundred historic watercrafts, including four National Historic Landmark vessels, most notably the 1841 whaleship *Charles W. Morgan*, America's oldest commercial ship still in existence.

Left: Walking the grounds of the nation's leading maritime museum. *Provided by Mystic Seaport Museum*

Opposite: A working shipyard at the Mystic Seaport Museum. *Courtesy of Mystic Seaport Museum*

While strolling through the historic village, visitors can learn firsthand from staff historians, storytellers, musicians, and craftspeople and discover just what life was like for those who earned their living from the sea. In the Henry B. du Pont Preservation Shipyard, they can watch shipwrights who are keeping the skills and techniques of traditional shipbuilding alive as they restore and maintain the museum's watercraft collection and other vessels.

The museum's 41,000-square-foot Collections Research Center (CRC) offers exceptional physical and electronic access to more than two million artifacts. The collections range from marine paintings, scrimshaw, models, tools, and ships' plans to an oral-history archive, extensive film and video recordings, and more than one million photographs. The CRC is also home to the G. W. Blunt White Library, a 75,000-volume research library where scholars from around the world come to study America's maritime history.

TAKE IT

Explore in a mini powerboat with **Mystic Boat Adventures—**
45 Pearl Street, Noank, Groton

Get on a mini powerboat to explore Fishers Island Sound, local lighthouses, and the Connecticut, New York, and Rhode Island waterways. You can even catch a glimpse of Taylor Swift's Rhode Island home, since trips can cover 20–25 miles over the course of one to three hours. Getting out on the water in these two-seater boats has become a bucket list experience for many. The experience is like go-karting on water, and the boats are controlled like a jet ski. Navigate the Mystic River through historic landmarks, the Mystic Seaport, and the drawbridge that will lead you out into the open water. The boats are great for thrill seeking or a relaxing cruise on the water to enjoy the sunset.

Mini powerboating into the sunset (*opposite*). There's never a dull moment on the waters between New York, Connecticut, and Rhode Island (*right*). *Courtesy of Kaylee Wright*

🏨 CHECKING IN

Foxwoods Resort Casino—*350 Trolley Line Boulevard, Mashantucket*

Foxwoods Resort Casino offers lodging, gaming, and much more. *Courtesy of Foxwoods Resort Casino*

Just a short drive from Mystic and Interstate 95 is the largest resort casino in North America. The property is a premier destination with an award-winning golf course, a waterpark, state-of-the art theaters, and (of course) a vast array of gaming in seven casinos. Since 1992, Foxwoods Resort Casino has been owned and operated by the Mashantucket Pequot Tribal Nation and has been a convenient getaway for New Englanders as a staycation or day outing.

MAKE IT

Handcraft a souvenir at **Nautical Arts Workshop**—
1 Meadow Woods Road, Deep River

Nautical Arts Workshop founder Peter McKenna is a handyman who spent much of his younger years as a boater on the local bays and harbors, sparking an obsession with the seafaring arts. He has taken his passion into the classroom, teaching woodworking to people of all ages. In 2001, he built a classroom barn, where he now hosts instructional courses on making wooden crafts, such as chests, cutting boards, and paddles.

The sea chest is perhaps the most familiar of all nautical furniture. Made usually by the sailor himself, it would have been one of his most important possessions. Not only did it store a sailor's personal belongings, but it also was the sailor's own particular nook on board a ship. It served as his table, his chair, his bank, and his bureau. These chests also gave a sailor an opportunity for personal expression through carvings, paintings, and decorations. The sea chests that Pete creates incorporate many design elements found in period sea chests. The chest is made of hand-planed eastern white pine. The front and back are canted and assembled with dovetail joinery. The overhanging top is supported by large iron strap hinges. The interior has a till and a brass lock, which is finished off with an ivory escutcheon. Hardwood cleats with a hand-carved star hold rope grommets tied with a shroud knot and finished with marline twine.

Since Connecticut's major pastime and competitive sport is undoubtedly rowing, there's no better souvenir to leave with than a custom-made oar to hang on your wall. Book a private lesson or join an ongoing woodworking class to design and carve your own rowing paddle or any other item you can make in a day, such as a birdhouse buoy or a ditty box. Call 860-767-7345 or send an email to info@thenauticalartsworkshop.com to make arrangements.

A handcrafted rowing oar is a perfect souvenir to hang on your wall. *Courtesy of Peter McKenna*

CHAPTER 13

GREENWICH, CONNECTICUT

Located west of New Haven toward the suburbs of New York City, Greenwich (pronounced "gren-ich") is a place where yacht clubs are abundant and the high-society network strives to impress one another. The town has four beaches on Long Island Sound, where you can enjoy swimming, boating, fishing, or relaxing on the

sand. Several festivals take place throughout the year for all interests—spotlighting arts, film, food, and other cultural subjects. Take a stroll through Greenwich's downtown, where you can enjoy fine dining, shops, and other attractions.

Downtown Greenwich. *Courtesy of the Connecticut Office of Tourism*

Blue Bloods on the Gold Coast

This coastal town is the largest on Connecticut's "Gold Coast"—a nickname it earned due to its many hedge funds and large financial service companies. As you can imagine, many of its residents commute into New York City for work via train. This blue-blooded community is home to two of the wealthiest zip codes in the state, 06830 and 06831, with average adjusted gross incomes of $638,560 and $721,550 and median household incomes of $109,250 and $155,417, respectively.

It's a place to bask in the life in and near the Long Island Sound, with a number of grassy coves, harbors, and rocky islands. You'll be introduced to the life of luxury and elitism and a community that prides itself on special access.

 ## WHAT IS A YACHT?

The word "yacht" comes from Dutch origin and was originally defined as a light and fast sailing vessel used by the Dutch navy to find and capture pirates. Some say it comes from the Dutch word "jaght," which was used to designate boats for pleasure by royalty. When King Charles II of England was carried by "jaght" from the Netherlands back home, in 1660, the word soon came to mean a vessel in which important people were carried, not just any old boat. Now, these recreational boats or ships range from 35 feet to more than 160 feet in length. Due to their large size, yachts can sail in deep ocean waters and withstand turbulent conditions. High-tech electronics and guiding instruments are more suitable for longer voyages. Conducting a yacht typically takes a full crew to help with navigation, maintenance, electronics and engineering, and repairs, and to serve as stewards to cater to the passengers. Yachts can be powered by either sails or motors with as much as 800 horsepower.

TAKE IT

Visit a storied social hub at **Indian Harbor Yacht Club**—
710 Steamboat Road

Founded by a group of prominent sportsmen in 1889, Indian Harbor Yacht Club has a long and storied tradition based on private yachts and pleasure boats. Their mission "shall be to encourage and support the sport of yachting, the art of yacht designing and building, and the science of seamanship and navigation and to provide for the amusement and recreation of its members." Take a tour of the property, from the harbor to the clubhouse, which shows off its nautically inspired decor and ambience. This yacht club is one of the most prestigious clubs in the area, where membership waiting lists are as long as a lifetime. Members have straight access to Captain Harbor on the western Long Island Sound, where three distinct cultures of boaters collide: sailors, powerboaters (known as stinkpots), and paddlers. Yacht clubs are social hubs for the boating community that offer a family-friendly atmosphere, team events, and competition. Call 203-869-2484 to schedule a tour. They would like a one-week notice in advance.

DIFFERENT TYPES OF ROWING: SCULLING AND SWEEP ROWING

What started as a transportation method in ancient Greece, Rome, and Egypt has since turned into a popular sport in America: rowing. Rowing is the first team sport contested in the US and continues to be a popular competitive sport among many schools. There are two types of rowing events: sculling and sweep rowing.

Athletes with two oars—one in each hand—are scullers. Generally, there are three sculling events: the single—1x (one person), the double—2x (two people), and the quad—4x (four people).

Athletes with only one oar are sweep rowers. Sweep boats may or may not carry a coxswain (pronounced "cox-n") to steer and be the on-the-water coach. In boats without coxswains, one of the rowers steers by moving the rudder with his or her foot. Sweep rowers come in pairs with a coxswain (2+) and pairs without (2−), fours with a coxswain (4+) and fours without (4−), and a crew of eight (8+), which always carries a coxswain. The eight is the fastest boat on the water. A world-level men's eight is capable of moving almost 14 miles per hour.

Opposite: Indian Harbor Yacht Club. *Courtesy of the Connecticut Office of Tourism*

Right: Early morning paddle on the Cos Cob Harbor. *Courtesy of Susan Magnamo*

Greenwich Water Club.
Courtesy of Susan Magnamo

TAKE IT

Train like an athlete at **Greenwich Water Club**—
49 River Road, Cos Cob

Professional rowers make the sport seem effortless. Most of us familiarize ourselves with rowing when tuning into the Olympic Games. Watching the synchronization of the crews embodies the meaning of teamwork, referencing inspirational posters displayed in conference rooms across America and popularized in the '90s. Greenwich Water Club's highly acclaimed programs are a source of those ideals: teamwork and self-discipline. In the boathouse, rowers train with nationally recognized Greenwich Crew coaches. You'll find professional and recreational rowers at dusk, working with personal trainers, taking fitness and yoga classes, and using an array of equipment. Their boating programs offer members club boats, kayaks, and stand-up paddleboards.

Experience a session with a rowing crew. Warm up on the rowing machines inside the fitness center, grab your oars, and jump onto a shell. If you're curious about what the difference is between an oar and a paddle, an oar is connected to the vessel by an oarlock and pin, whereas a paddle is held completely by the rower. Oars contain a single blade and propel the craft in the opposite direction of the rower, giving the feeling of traveling backward. A big heads-up: rowing out on the water is nothing like the machine. Twisting the oars takes a lot of practice, especially in coordination with other rowers on your boat. If the oar's blade doesn't dip into the water at the right angle, then it jumps back and jerks. To embrace the challenge, schedule an appointment with coach Darren Gary at least one month in advance by emailing dgary@greenwichwaterclub.com.

INTERVIEW WITH COACH DARREN GARY OF THE GREENWICH ROWING TEAM

What was your upbringing to discover rowing?

I was born in Texas and went to boarding school for high school in Chattanooga, Tennessee. It was an all-boys school that comprised kids from twenty-eight states and sixteen countries. The curriculum focused on leadership, responsibility, and citizenship. We were taught strong emotional-social skills through extracurricular activity. A coach approached me to be a part of the rowing team, since basketball took a different skill set that I didn't have. The schedule was demanding, but I learned hard work, patience, and discipline. This prepared me to excel at the collegiate level, where I continued in the sport and into my coaching role.

Why do you think the sport is associated with the upper class and Ivy League institutions?

Contrary to popular belief, rowing is a pretty diverse sport that reaches across all socioeconomic classes. There are programs like Row New York that are accessible to inner-city youths in the Bronx and Harlem. Rowboats are provided for anyone that wants to be a part of a team. It's not a glamorous sport that many kids are attracted to, so it does take a certain type of personality and drive. Much of the training does involve being indoors on a rowing machine, but the real magic happens when you're out on the water.

How does the sport help people with their professional life?

There's lots of carryover, like great character and the quality of a person. I think it does attract like-minded people that are goal oriented and want to get out on the water to push themselves. People here will hire other people that row. There's a camaraderie to the sport, since people get up before the sun, knock out a killer workout, and start your day with mental clarity. The rest of the day becomes a breeze since you net a big win for the day.

What are the biggest challenges for a beginner?

Sticking with it. Patience is a must because it is proven that you get better over time, and it doesn't matter your age. We have athletes that improve their times in their fifties. But the sport is a grind, especially on the rowing machine. It's all worth it when you get out into nature and the world around you feels still.

Darren Gary coaching his rowing squad from a mini powerboat.
Courtesy of Susan Magnamo

⊙ WHILE YOU'RE HERE

Before you depart, you should discover that Greenwich is known to be a city of special access, but downtown's **Greenwich Avenue** is inviting, filled with outdoor restaurants along the sidewalks, shopping, and boutique shops. Explore the elaborate neighborhoods anywhere you drive. If you want to stay on the water, a drive through Old Greenwich to **Greenwich Point Park** is open to the public. There are a few local businesses that rent out paddleboats, or you can just enjoy the beach.

Downtown Greenwich. *Courtesy of the Connecticut Office of Tourism*

CHAPTER 14

THE END OF THE SHORELINE

If you've managed not to get seasick while *Gettin' Nautical in New England*, it's a win—although, after the fact, even that experience can make for a great story. This stretch along Interstate 95 from Portland, Maine, to Greenwich, Connecticut, is only an approximately five-hour, 300-mile drive without distraction, but this journey proves that stopping to smell the roses—or, in this case, smell the sea breeze—is worth every additional minute.

As you travel, you can pay homage to the Pilgrams who forged a new world for freedom of ideas and beliefs. When the region was first settled, transportation was limited on land, making New England saturated and confined with historical events, established townships, and a shared culture. There's no other place in America that's as generationally rich as New England, and—as you've noticed through your travels along this route—there are a lot of people who haven't left, which ensures that traditions stand long and proud.

Some might measure wealth through monetary value, which is prevalent in pockets of New England, as seen from the brownstone townhomes of Boston to the cape-style mansions of Martha's Vineyard, but the riches that visitors value are the region's ties to its history and the modernization of its relationship to the waters. The commercialization of lobstering has created notoriety for Maine, the harbor waters of Massachusetts and Rhode Island allow a visit back in time, and the voyage out in the Long Island Sound extends affection for life into the water. It's impossible to imagine what life would be like in New England if the waters didn't exist.

What's key to keeping this territory of America relevant and respected a hundred years from now is the sharing of stories, and now—after your trip through New England's nautical past and present—you are an interpreter who can share your experiences when you return home.

ABOUT YOUR GUIDE

Daniel Seddiqui is a multitime international bestselling author, inspiring keynote speaker, and educational and travel entrepreneur. His unwavering curiosity and love of people has led him to him being dubbed "the Most Traveled Person in American History" as he discovers the country in uncharted ways that focus on various careers, cultures, and environments.

Daniel is widely known for working jobs in all fifty states, writing a book about the experience (*50 Jobs in 50 States*) and becoming an inspiration to millions struggling with economic hardship and self-identity. He has appeared on and in countless international media outlets, such as CNN, Fox News, *Psychology Today*, TIME Inc., MSNBC, NPR, the *Today* show, *World News Tonight*, the *Wall Street Journal*, *Newsweek*, *USA Today*, and many others. His work speaks to those who yearn for growth and discovery and who want to lead with purpose and impact. Daniel's message is an example of perseverance, risk taking, adaptability, networking, and endurance. He lives in Bend, Oregon.

For more information on Daniel, including details on the organized tours he leads for those interested in traveling with a group, visit www.livingthemap.com.